DONALD M. JOY, Ph.D., is Professor of Human Development and occupies the Ray and Mary Jo West Chair of Christian Education at Asbury Theological Seminary in Wilmore, Kentucky. He is noted for his writing and speaking in the areas of sexual integrity and bonding. The author of many books, he has also written *Walk On!* for Victor Books.

UNFINISHED
BUSINESS

UNFINISHED
BUSINESS

DONALD JOY

VICTOR BOOKS ®

A DIVISION OF SCRIPTURE PRESS PUBLICATIONS INC.
USA CANADA ENGLAND

Recommended Dewey Decimal Clas-
sification: 155.632
Suggested Subject Heading: DIFFEREN-
TIAL AND GENETIC PSYCHOLOGY: MEN

Library of Congress Catalog Number:
89-60163
ISBN: 0-89693-275-9

Contents

Dedication

To the Men in Formation and Support Groups
with me at Asbury Theological Seminary
1972–1989

Craig Adams, Carey Akin, Terry Alderson, Jim Allen, Rick Alnutt, David Anderson, Joe Aurand, David Ashworth, John Baird, David Ballinger, Carey Balzer, David Barton, Sam Bartlett, Bob Beebe, Pat Bennett, Randy Bennett, Greg Bentle, Dennis Blackwell, Steve Blakemore, Dan Boyd, Tim Bracken, John Britt, Bob Brothers, David Brownlee, Ed Bryson, Kent Byer, Bobby Cain, Mark Cain, Walter Carter, Shelly Caulder, Rick Charles, Mike Childs, Kurt Church, J.P. Clark, Jay Clark, Glen Clark, Rick Clyde, Gary Coates, Jerry Coleman, Jack Connell, David Cotton, Kevin Crawford, Doug Cross, Jay Crouse, Todd Danningburg, Casey Davis, Jerry Davis, Wesley Davis, Marty DeBow, Doug Diehl, Jay Dudley, Jeff Dunn, Maurice "Mo" Dunn, Ken Edwards, David Ellis, Hon Eng, Steve Englehardt, Jeff Fellman, Dan Ferguson, Mark Filonczuk, Brian Fink, Chris Fisher, Jeff Ford, Ben Foulk, David Fowler, Derin Fowler, John Fowler, Larry Fowler, Tom Fraley, Sam Fritz, Mac Fulcher, Doug Gamble, Greg Gibson, Terry Gibson, Randy Gillett, Rick Givens, Grant Graff, Larry Green, Greg Groves, Greg Hanks, Jack Hankins, Dirk Hansen, Casey Harding, Tom Hauschild, Gary Hawkins, Bruce Hayes, Buff Hearn, Kent Hedlund, Glenn Hendrix, Wayne Henegar, Dan Hines, Mike Hinton, Wayne Hepler, Steve Heyduck, Chris Hill, Phil Hogg, David Hodge, Audie Hodges, Jon Honda, Jeff Horton, John Hubbs, Bill Hughes, Dick Huston, Wes Irwin, Jonathan Isaacs, Vic Johnson, Gary Jones, Rob Jones, Tom Kalina, Jim Kane, Mark Kennedy, Wayne Kenney, Evan Kenyon, Chris Kiesling, Tom Kilburn, Charlie Krueger, David Kubal, Mendall Kugler, Pete Legner, Mike Lehman, John LeMasters, Scott Leu, Phil Lewis, Greg Ligon, Dale Locke, Steve Logsdon, John Long, Bill Love, Ken Love, Dan Lutz, Mark Mac Adow, Jerry Massie, Dan Maurer, Mike Maxey, Gerry McCall, David McCarthy, Billy McCauley, David McConnell, G.J. McGarvey, Mel McGinnis, Wes McIntyre, Rodney McKean, Tim McKinney, Stan McKinnon, Bruce McLaughlin, Larry Mealy, David Meddars, Ralph Merante, Tom Michalko, Gil Miller, Jonathan Moore, Lynn Moore, Matt Mote, Michael Mudge, Gary Mulholland, David Murray, Randy Miller, David Moehring, Richard Monroe, Carl Morton, Rob Nicholson, Terry Otto, Jonathan Palmer, David Panther, Dan Parry, Randy Pasqua, Johnny Patterson, Steve Pescosolido, "Luch" Pope, David Powless, Sam Price , Bill Quick, Benjamin "Bo" Quigg, John Rech, Alan Retzman, Frank Reynolds, Don Richards, Shan Ricketts, Ed Ross, Mike Schneider, Steve Seamands, Bill Seitz, Michael Shea, Rick Sheppard, Jack Shields, Brian Shimer, Lynn Shmidt, Craig Sider, Duane Skene, T.J. Slocum, Brian Small, Brad Smith, Brian Smith, Dan Smith, Daryl Smith, Dean Smith, Eric Smith, Tim Smith, Steve Somers, Don Spachman, Gordon Sparks, Tom Strickfaden, Jack Strong, David Swarbrick, Dean Taylor, Kevin Thompson, Mark Tidman, Ivan "Ike" Timm, Adrian Timmons, Jim Tysick, Christian Ulrich, Kent Usry, Doug Vogel, Mel Vostry, Bill Wade, Mark Wade, Steve Waldorf, John Walt, Ron Waughter, Danny Wayman, Dennis Wayman, Steve Wenzel, Carl Westbrook, Ryan Wickman, Gene Williams, Greg Wood, Larry Wright, Dean Ziegler

Foreword

When the manuscript for *Unfinished Business: How a Man Can Make Peace with His Past* arrived, its title sparked a twinge of curiosity mixed with anxiety. The table of contents seemed dangerously relevant to my own pilgrimage. It occurred to me that this scholar in the field of human development, writing about the male pilgrimage experience, had known me personally all of my adult life. Could it be, I wondered anxiously, that he has been analyzing me for twenty-five years and is now going to report to the whole world what he knows about me? Or has he some special insight to wider dynamics of male development and experience?

When Donald Joy first joined Ellen and me for Sunday dinner in Toronto, we were newlyweds. Although I didn't know it at the time, I was immersed in the throes of my "age-twenty transition." Daniel Levinson hadn't yet written his *Seasons of a Man's Life* but, nevertheless, I was at that critical intersection of male development. Joy seemed to understand me in that first meeting in ways that I did not know myself. His affirmation, modeling, and exhortation moved Ellen and me more deeply into our marriage and more deeply into our trust of him. Intermittent contacts across those next years found us visiting in Indiana, Toronto, and in Rochester, New York. It sounded "too good to be true" when I learned that he would offer "The Teaching Methods of Jesus" during my last semester at Asbury Seminary. Dr. Joy had been drafted to teach, on an emergency interim basis, to cover the course load of a professor who had died during the Christmas holiday. That course title mattered less than the fact that this man would again touch my life.

In retrospect, I now enjoy the observation that I was headed naively into my "age-thirty transition." I was changing, and once again, Don Joy was there to shepherd me through a significant passage. He was helping me to reflect on the values of Jesus. Joy was living out a life of wholeness. He was teaching by example the worthy styles of life and ministry I needed to see as well as hear. And now I know, though I did not know it then, that he was rescuing several of us from the slippery path heading toward superficiality, theatrical styles of ministry, isolation, and things false.

I walked away with a grade, a final semester ended, and a diploma announcing my "Master of Divinity" credential. That chapter of my relationship with Don ended, but the good providence of God caused our paths to cross from time to time. That is why my appointment in 1976, to pastor the Wilmore, Kentucky, Free Methodist congregation seemed a little overwhelming. Dr. Donald M. Joy would be a member of the congregation. How, I wondered, does one go about shepherding a mentor?

Sensing, perhaps, my hesitation, Don freely gave me permission to be his pastor. I had expected that a person of his stature might go elsewhere for significant pastoral care. But on more than one occasion, he surprised me by exposing growing edges and asking for the "care of the soul."

Authenticity characterized every side of this Christian statesman. His commitment to the kind of integrity that had characterized his expanding ministry across the continent was evident in his relationships within the local church. We worked together. We prayed together. We shared burdens and we shared pain. I was developing as a person, and he was also developing, and we could both affirm that growth as we walked ahead surrounded by God's transforming grace.

By the time I hit my "age-forty transition," I was hundreds of miles from Dr. Joy, and deeply mired in "midlife crisis." I was the father of three sons, the pastor of forty pastors, and a member of a denominational leadership team that was seeking to enrich and guide the life of the church. Professionally successful, I was nonetheless out of touch with some basic realities of God's vision for adult males who are husbands, fathers, and responsible men.

Not unlike other men, I later discovered that I had meandered into adulthood weighed down with interpersonal naivete, affective paralysis, emotional deafness, and the corresponding inability to respond with interpersonal warmth. One day, quite unexpectedly, an interpersonal earthquake jolted our marriage and awakened me to my unwholeness. Ellen immediately phoned Donald Joy.

I think it was his unconditional commitment to integrity as well as his understanding of the unseen agenda in human life that moved her to make that call. When Ellen hung up, we cleared our schedules, farmed out the kids, and headed for the Joy home in Kentucky. Within twenty-four hours, as Professor Joy came and went to classes and other obligations, we began to work our way through personality profiles, listening sessions, and candid sharing. Ever so slowly, the light began to dawn. I will forever be indebted to Ellen for that unusual stroke of insight and the energy and grace she mustered to make the call.

All of that is history. Our marriage has moved out of shadows into sunlight, out of isolation into communion, and out of silence into sharing. We date much of that growth to the forty-eight hours we spent with Don and

Robbie as I faced the deep agendas of my "age-forty transition."

Now with this new manuscript on my desk, I know this is the book I needed before my wedding day in August of 1965. It would have answered so many questions and calmed so many fears. I could have moved much more rapidly and with greater assurance toward maturity in loving and in fathering had I had this handbook—*Unfinished Business: How a Man Can Make Peace with His Past*. Every week I work with men who are at various critical moments common among males of our species. I need this book today.

I've parsed every verb in Don's recent books. My story is woven through all of his books, or so it seems to me. This latest one comes again with the stunning candor that men really need. Some books tell what we already know and stop where they should begin. Here is real grist for real men in real life. This book begins where most men are—caught in the web of realities for which they have no vocabulary or tools of thought.

I commend *Unfinished Business* not just for its scholarly treatment of data, though I am impressed with the thoroughness of the analysis. I do not praise it because of the personal support which Dr. Joy has been to me, though I would go far to do him a favor. I commend the book as the truth that sets men free. These concepts are life-changing, marriage-changing, and liberating beyond belief.

Men, read for your life!

Dr. Gary R. Walsh, Pastor
Pearce Memorial Free Methodist Church
Rochester, New York

Introduction

"My name is Ralph, and I need to tell you that I don't know what I am doing here. Six months ago when I was teaching school I thought I knew why I was coming to seminary. But last night I was devastated with feelings I can't understand. Cathy was really worried. She should have been, I guess. As I drove around for about an hour last night I actually planned my own death. So I know I'm in trouble. When Dr. Joy asked if I wanted to join a lunch hour group, I knew I needed some help. When I told him just fifteen minutes ago about last night, he said he hoped I would share it with you now."

As Ralph unfolded his story of immediate personal need, his vulnerability and desperation were an instant catalyst for a group meeting the first time. A week later, when I asked the group to reflect on that "introduction" to the men's support network, Mel responded with big eyes and wild gestures: "I wondered what I had got myself into! When Ralph opened his feelings and told that awful stuff he was going through, I thought, man alive! If everybody is going to share at that level, I don't know whether I can face the music. I'm not ready to lay my whole naked life on the line like that." But in time, Mel did, and continues to share in an alumni group that meets annually for a great marathon session.

Before I came to teach at Asbury Seminary I accumulated forty-three years of experience growing up male and negotiating life reasonably well. As I reflected back, however, I could name only a half dozen men who really "knew" me at any moment. Most of them populated quartets with whom I traveled on weekends for Central College in Kansas, Greenville College in Illinois, and Asbury Seminary between 1945 and 1954. It was the accumulated time trapped in automobiles en route to concerts that reduced us to transparency with each other. Even today, whenever I can catch a moment face-to-face or by phone with one of those men, I realize how important they were in my personal development. The weekend concert tours typically locked us into twenty-four-hour-per-day contact with each other.

Those saturation experiences have helped me to design intensive ministry events such as the "discipleship development through trail camping" curriculum which combines backpacking with lightly structured sharing of life stories. We say "the trail is the curriculum," and we watch "community" happen. The support networks I facilitate on campus in the brown-bag lunch hour groups focus on accumulated time with intentional attention to ourselves and our stories.

Unfinished Business: How a Man Can Make Peace with His Past could never have been written had I not been immersed in male support groups for the last eighteen years. When I began teaching at Asbury in 1971, I did some quick reflection on maintaining professional distance and avoiding the tendency to pick favorites. I reminisced about a seminary professor who had always called his students by their last name with a prefix of Mister. That seemed plausible between my ears, but I found that I was too eager to know my students informally to keep such a distance through the use of titles.

It was Wayne Kenney, in the spring of 1971, and Rodney McKean in the fall of 1972, who formed me into a

professor I could never have become without their prod-
ding. Wayne broke the professional barrier by looking
after my week-by-week needs as a "commuting professor," right down to collecting the free TV schedule distributed at the local grocery store. Rodney initiated the
request that led to the first lunch-hour group. That group
and its successors met daily in the dining commons for
about four years. Eventually we moved to my office to
avoid the conspicuous visibility of professor and students meeting daily over lunch. But the visibility did not
solve another professional and ethical question for me:
How do I invest significant time in a few students without arousing feelings of rejection or jealousy among
those who feel outside of my priority time?

The answer was in publishing a roster which hangs on
the bulletin board outside my office. It lists names of
participants and weekly schedules of meeting times. Not
more than four people each semester inquire about how
to get into a group. And the number of men graduating
or needing to leave runs about the same number.

I am now free to accept a wonderful fact: nobody can
sustain an infinite number of quality relationships.
Either we will choose to live in chilling anonymity to
everyone, or we will take E. Mansell Pattison's "rule,"
and look for twenty to thirty significant friendships in
which we may invest intentional time. These "significant others" are a dynamic set, changing as life's circumstances change.

Long-distance relationships are difficult to nurture. I
was relieved to find that people who try to write regularly after space separates them, eventually turn out to
be neurotic. A major investment in cross-country friendships cuts into time needed to make contact in your
present world. Long-distance correspondence simply
does not nourish the spirit and keep one sane in the way
that face-to-face contacts do.

So my sanity and spiritual wellness across the last
twenty years is largely a gift from these students who

have entered into my life and allowed me to enter into theirs—always in the presence of a witnessing and supporting community of brothers.

You will find names of most of those men in the dedication of this book. I shudder at the omissions, of which there may be as many as a dozen. But my records are incomplete and my memory is that of an absent-minded professor. I am eager to hear from anyone who may know who the missing people are. My memo file seems to begin in about 1978. Before that time, we evidently did all scheduling orally in the lunch hour circle. I suspect that the first memo originated when I ventured into multiple groups. Today, in three groups—Tuesday, Thursday, and Friday lunch hours—I see a total of thirty-six men each week. In the spring of 1986, my wife (Robbie) and I took forty-eight men and their wives and dates to a steak-night dinner in the dining commons. That must have been the largest group.

These men have taught me how complicated they are. But they have also proved how easy it is for men to tell the truth about their experiences when they (a) invest time with a stable group, and (b) accept an invitation to talk about themselves.

The secrets shared here are composites of real stories or are carefully placed behind the protection of first-name-only synonyms. I am indebted to a dozen of the men whose stories are unique. They have given consent to the final draft of their stories in the manuscript.

In *Unfinished Business* I am walking around the amazing collection of discoveries these hundreds of good men have opened up with me singly and in groups. I have opened windows into my own childhood, into adolescent pain and rejection, and have shown the probable connection with my life-long vulnerability to walk with anybody else through their pain. The early college years, with the listening they brought, lavishly rewarded by vaulting me into campus-elected leadership, was a first clue that I was custodian of a gift.

Introduction

Peers, as well as older and younger men, have sensed that I was at least willing to contemplate the darkest and most humiliating of their agonies. Louis Shirey and Mike Reynolds, early in my Asbury career, tested my mettle with questions I had never faced in the same way before. For each, I begged for time to locate resources I did not then have.

My lifetime of experiences has led me to examine the mystery of what it means to be born male, the high demands we place on fathers and mothers, and the search for independent identity during the adolescent years. Then, in the search for intimacy with a woman, chapters unfold the "way it is supposed to be," followed by three chapters which describe things that go wrong—male inclinations to "hide" behind the macho facade, or to feed an appetite for polygyny and multiple partners. The chapter on men and marital risk describes typical problems in which men become enmeshed, with offers of help and recovery for the marriage. Chapter Eleven offers suggestions for getting men the networks and support they need, including agendas I have used with men's spiritual formation groups. Finally, I provide a "certificate of permission" for men who want to thrive: "Join the 'E-J-B' Club." It validates the need to ask real questions in a high-fidelity, fully sober environment of trusted peers. This is what all men are looking for; this is what all men need.

ONE

◇

BORN
TO BE A MAN

I was thirteen years old when Mother and Dad brought home a new baby brother. My sister had been born when I was seven, and we had waited another six years for the third child to be born. I was eager to make his acquaintance. But shortly after I had picked him up out of the crib and begun to carry him around the house, he suddenly was "wet." I took him into the kitchen where Mother was making the first meal since her return home. Where else do you take a wet baby except to its mother?

"He's wet," I said.

"You can change his diaper. Bring me a clean one from the bedroom, and I'll show you how to fold it."

So within a couple of minutes I was carrying him to the guest room bed, with a freshly folded diaper under my arm. Placing him on the bed, I carefully removed the safety pins. When the diaper fell away I was startled. My baby brother had a fresh scar running from the base of his penis full circle vertically around his scrotum! *He's been cut!* I thought. The scar was so straight, it looked like it had been made with a knife. Red, bright, and fresh, it stood up in a ridge of freshly healed flesh, and extended up the bottom side of his tiny penis.

I was angry, flushed with resentment toward Doc Adams, who must have cut him. Growing up on a farm, I knew about such cuttings of male animals, and I was angry. But I looked carefully, then reasoned it out: there are no stitches, so Doc Adams didn't do it.

The scar was a mystery. I closed the fresh diaper and said nothing to anyone. But the bright red scar bothered me. I saw it often, and soon after when it occurred to me to examine myself, I discovered that I carried an almost invisible matching mark. Not until I was past the age of fifty would I find an explanation for my little brother's scar so fresh and red.

THE MALE PHENOMENON

Eventually I changed a few other diapers, including those of our two sons, and eventually our three grandsons. The same bright red scar was always there. It was there from the moment of birth. I was confident we were not dealing with a saber-happy doctor tampering with male genitals. Physicians, if they knew where the scar came from, weren't telling our family, and we hadn't the courage to ask questions.

Indeed, we didn't know sexual anatomy well enough to ask intelligent questions. When physicians talked, they spoke in Latin names anyway. Who of us was competent to carry on a conversation with a highly trained professional? Anyway, the typical doctor's response was, "it is nothing to worry about." So the scar remained a mystery to me.

I had never given a second thought to the fact that baby boys have breasts. Adult men have nipples, of course, exactly positioned where female breasts are. You can't tell a baby boy from a baby girl with a diaper on, because the upper bodies look identical. Boys aren't born with whiskers. Only the genitals are different. Up to the age of ten or so, if the hairstyle and clothing are ambiguous, a boy's body looks just like a girl's. When I finally learned the amazing truth about how boys and girls are formed in the mother's womb, I was shocked, but somehow prepared.

The truth is that only the chromosomes are different. Any girl might have turned out to be a boy, and any boy might have gone on to be a girl if it hadn't been for the father's chromosome contribution. His sperm carried the sex-determining chromosome, and buried itself in the mother's egg. The old *King James Version* referred to it as the "seed" of the woman (Gen. 3:15). A male provides about three million energetic sperm in every sexual contact with a female. The sperm defy gravity and move up through the cervix, through the uterus, and on into the fallopian tubes in search of an unsuspecting egg which may have been recently released during ovulation. If an egg is available to those sperm, one of the sperm will "strike" first and bury its head in the egg. That pierced ovum then moves out of the tube and into the uterus. There it finds a suitable place to hook up to the wall where it will grow into the full term baby, eventually releasing and passing through the mouth of the uterus, the cervix, and down the vaginal tract. The new baby completes this trip through the birth canal, and bursts out into the world and into our arms.

If the father's implanting sperm carries an X chromosome it matches the mother's chromosome which is always X—always female. It is that mother's X chromosome that determines the basic body configuration. The baby's basic structure is female: breasts, ovaries, vagina—the works! But if the father's implanting sperm carries a Y chromosome, it overpowers the X decision, but not until after the basic body is formed. Then the Y chromosome gives the orders: "Customize this baby. Make it a male." But it is always a "modification" command, so the basic model of the baby during the first trimester is that of the female. Indeed, if a baby boy were lost through miscarriage or abortion during that first trimester, it would *appear to be a female*. All babies look the same during that phase of development, even though development is highly complex. For example, the baby has fingernails by this time. And if you were to examine the lost baby boy, you would see an open vagina to match those breasts! What is more, if you were to see a cross section of the sex organs inside that baby's body, it would have two easily identifiable ovaries.

WHEN ADAM SPLITS

It has been a painful discovery for me, well past mid-life, to discover that I misunderstood the doctrine of Creation. I had thought, all of my life, that God created a bachelor male and called him Adam. Now, forced by the sheer startling truth of human conception and development to reexamine the Genesis account, I discovered that the same story is told there:

1. God created a solitary human, named Adam.
2. The solitary, though complete, state was "not good," because the human was alone.
3. God created community by forming woman and man from the same Adam.

Genesis 5 summarizes the whole thing and tells us straightforwardly, God created them male and female, He blessed them, and called them Adam. Fortunately, it is the *New International Version* that has the courage to tell us this, if only in a footnote.[1] It turns out that "they" are Adam, "male and female," and the Genesis 2 description is of the "splitting of the Adam" into male and female: properly called "sexually differentiating" the human species.

So Creation revisits every conception, and the chromosomes determine which half of the split to follow. Human sexual differentiation was not given to us by God because it was necessary for human reproduction. The original Adam was complete. But sexual differentiation was provided by the scalpel of God in a surgical separation of female and male. The reason? God saw that "it is not good for the *Adam* [my translation] to be alone" (Gen. 2:18).

When I first coined the term "splitting the Adam" to describe what God did surgically in Genesis 2, I thought I was capitalizing on nuclear language to generate a bit of humor. Imagine my surprise to learn that the word atom was brought into English from the same biblical material. The word often translated "dust of the earth" is *adamah*, and in the doctrine of creation it speaks always of the close linkage of our humanity with the raw material of the planet. So atom and Adam both come from the Creation language: one for the human formed of the dust, and the other referring to the minutest particles of Creation material!

The ovary-looking pair of sexual organs in the undifferentiated baby will become ovaries in the female and testicles in the male. The mother's own chemicals, notably her trace of male hormones (androgens), are attracted by the XY chromosome baby to the ovary-looking organs. These ducts, which will become the fallopian tubes in the female, serve as the transportation tunnel by which the testicles are moved from inside the body to the external location in the scrotum. These "testicles in process" are coated with a chemical wrapping, broken loose, and drawn into the fallopian tubes. The strong chemistry destroys the fallopian tubes even while they are conveying the new testicles to their exterior sac home. But two traces of the basic female system remain in the adult male:

1. The top ends appear as an "appendix" with the testicles.
2. The lower end, which will become the female uterus, dangles in the urinary tract and is technically called the "prostatic utricle" or "vestigal uterus." Some medical authorities suggest that this leftover uterus is part of the complication for later life male prostate problems.

The testicles, which might have continued to develop

as ovaries, will be transformed into a pair of sperm producing factories which will turn out up to three hundred million sperm per day for most of adult life. Immediately upon their alteration they begin to produce distinctly male hormones, including the powerful testosterone. This testosterone production is credited with the fact that mothers carrying a baby boy tend to experience more vigorous fetal movement than those carrying a baby girl.

The vaginal lips seal slowly to form the amazing "straight as a knife" red scar. The vaginal lips therefore form the sac or scrotum which houses the testicles. Their external location is essential for cooling the factories which produce sperm. Sperm will not be healthy and fertile unless they are produced at a temperature about three degrees below normal body temperature. Those vaginal lips provide the thermostatic and elastic skin which provides the testicles with a retractable sac. That same amazing skin also envelopes the penis making possible its inflation during erection. No skin anywhere else on the body has the flexibility of this vaginal lip material which, in the male, is transformed to scrotum and penis covering.

In cold weather the scrotum contracts and pulls the testicles up tightly against the body, but in warm weather the scrotum drops the testicles further from the body in order to maintain a constant correct temperature for developing healthy and fertile sperm. But the same elastic material from the vaginal lips forms the sheath of skin which encloses the developing penis—hence the red scar which continues from the scrotum up the base of the penis. The penis is actually the clitoris transformed and enlarged by androgens to develop a shaft. As the vaginal lips enfold the penis, the urinary tract is extended and enclosed just beneath the red scar. So the pleasure center in the originally female-formed body of the growing baby is now expanded and elevated to become the head of the penis shaft[2].

SINGLE-MINDED MALES

In my book, *Bonding: Relationships in the Image of God,* I have given detailed description and documentation about both genital and brain differentiation, but the brief descriptions here are essential if we are to understand the Creation gifts with which males arrive on this planet.

If the "common body" from which female and male emerge following conception and the first trimester of development strikes you as amazing, consider what happens to the human brain. Males and females are profoundly dependent on each other in understanding the real world, largely because the brain that sits between their ears is so different. If we called the genital formation phase of human development sexual differentiation because they turned into mirror images opposite to each other, then we must find a way to talk about brain differentiation.

The natural state of the human brain is female. Again we are confronted with the essentially female nature of our humanity. Every baby begins with a brain developed on the female model. There is an easy flow of neurological messages from one hemisphere to the other. "Ambihemisphere capability" would characterize all humans in that female configuration. But the male brain is modified again in response to the father's Y chromosome which has joined the mother's X. This combination calls for the chemicals to alter the genital system, and at the sixteenth week of the pregnancy, the mother's androgens are called into action again. This time they will "damage" and specialize the young boy's brain. The boy's own androgens, especially the testosterone from the tiny testicles which have already begun to produce, are also put to use in altering his own brain.

In a very selective way, the left hemisphere of the male brain is coated with the hormonal chemical. The corpus colossum, which consists of several millions of neurological fibers which join the two hemispheres, is also coated with a ten-week bath which will destroy a significant part of those "communication" links, greatly diminishing the young male's ability to simultaneously mix and coordinate the use of both hemispheres.

While the damage to the speech center, typically located in the left hemisphere of all right-handed folks, is easily the most obvious effect of this "in utero" modification of the boy's brain, it is no more important than several others.

Visual processing. Males tend to have superior ability to develop eye-hand coordination. They invent games of competition and historically have survived by this uncanny "developable" ability which undergirds all kinds of marksmanship. Today's male fascination with computer games and video parlor prowess may be the most conspicuous display of this gift. This skill development stems from a three-dimensional-perception ability that seems to develop more powerfully in males than in females. Not only may this gift show up in eye-hand coordination, but also in the superior ability to identify distance between oneself and an object suspended in air (eg., a clothesline). It is this endowment that thrusts male's almost magically into three-dimensional reasoning. While general arithmetic and math are basically two-dimensional, geometry, calculus, and other engineering-like higher maths require "inferential" reasoning based on the ability to "see" what is not visible. Standard IQ and SAT tests, which provide pictures of stacked oranges from which to infer the regular pattern and determine the number in the whole pile, measure this ability to do three-dimensional reasoning.

We may add to these male patterns of processing the additional feature of the female's reverse optic system in comparison to the male. She, for example, tends to suffer from night blindness after facing oncoming headlights, while he reaches for sunglasses in fighting daylight blindness. Here, as in so many ways, woman and man are mirrors of each other. Little wonder that as we contemplate the original Adam, it takes two to become one.

Reasoning. You can imagine that optical development affects how we gather information for thought. But once the information is in the brain, males tend to work it over in a single-minded way, using their logical and analytical processes. By largely shutting down their "feeling" hemisphere, men are able to concentrate in noisy environments, for example. When they are focused in this way, whether by choice or necessity, it may be very hard to "break through" their single-mindedness. Women, with the wonderfully undamaged corpus colossum, are more open to interruptions and more "whole-minded" in their responses. Music, prayer, and poetry put a man in his "right mind," so he is easier to "dialogue with" under conditions which have not flipped his switch into "single-hemisphere" mode.

Emotions. Men are more at the mercy of their feelings, since right-handed, right eye dominant men tend to speak from their logical analytical hemisphere. They do poorly at articulating their "right mind" where feelings, emotions, and noumenal beliefs are housed. Since men are often slower to articulate love, affection, or belief in supernatural, nonlogical dimensions of spiritual reality, they tend also to be less able to guard against assaults on and manipulation of their emotions. While men are characterized as being unemotional, at times of great loss it is not uncommon for them to lose control and be unable to explain what triggered the feelings.

Men are capable of high emotion and profound belief in the numinous—the transcendent spiritual realities—but they are often unable to communicate verbally in describing the experiences that mean so much to them. They frequently resort to musical composition or performance, or to painting, drawing, or writing in order to express this bottled-up numinous or affective experience. Most likely the arts have been dominated by males because of this single-minded verbal limitation and the resulting backlog of unexpressible experience which must be forced out through some medium.

Mapping. A lower rear lobe develops in the right hemisphere of males, sufficiently visible to allow sex identification if our brains were visible. This lump of highly developed brain tissue has been identified as the center from which males get their spatial orientation. The enlarged area in males is just below the hatband line, at the back of the right hemisphere.

Eskimo men are legendary for their ability to find their way across "white on white" terrain to their homes with incredible efficiency and accuracy. Males in our technological world may not have such a perfect record compared with their women, but any couple who has ever tried to meet at some geographic point will likely have learned that men and women image differently when they think of space and geography.

It is significant here too that this male capacity seems to be related to a segment of the right hemisphere—the one that most men have great difficulty putting into words. Their directional instincts are better acted out than reduced to words. For example, a man is more likely than a woman to draw a map if asked for directions.

Sexual attraction. When comparing males and females, perhaps less is known about the source of sexual orientation than any other of the brain's differences. Recent studies, reported at a conference on sexual differentiation in the brain, documented, in some research cases, the connection between homosexual preference and trauma suffered by the mother during the sixteenth to twenty-sixth week of pregnancy. The findings evoked a listing of two medical obligations: (1) Diagnosis and prevention of androgen deprivation during this critical ten-week period in mothers pregnant with males. (2) Remediation for males so affected by prenatal androgen deprivation.[3]

We have known for nearly forty years that male sexual orientation is more complex and falls into a less clear set of options than the female's. Evidently, the degree to which a baby's brain is masculinized varies from child to child. If so, then the strength or weakness of any group of males' sexual preference might be expected to extend across a spectrum, even if all were predominantly heterosexual in preference. When you add the possibility that an occasional baby boy might slip through during a period of serious hormonal depletion, either from stress or from ovarian overproduction of estrogens, you might expect to find a baby with male genitals but with a brain that remains essentially female. In Chapter 4, I will explore nurturing masculinity in boys, since growing up male seems to be a bit more hazardous than it is growing up female.

Since it is the brain that responds to the million stimuli that affect sexual response, we will not debate long about where sexual arousal begins. Jesus knew the brain was the most powerful sex organ when He cautioned about lust in the heart (Matt. 5:28). According to Jesus, mental or visual pursuit and desire to use a person's body for sexual pleasure amounts to emotional adultery. Evidently Jesus confronted the proud accusers of the woman caught in adultery in John 8 with the accusation of heart adultery. Today we know that sexual arousal is set off when the brain releases a chemical which instantly blocks the flow of blood away from the genitals and nipples. The tissues then become engorged with blood. They remain rigid and blood-inflated until the imagination passes or is interrupted.

Speech. It is common that nine out of ten children in the speech pathologist's special group are boys. While emotional trauma may leave effects in speech, and physiological malformation may account for others, the larger portion of cases are boys suffering from damaged speech development because of the prenatal androgen brain bath. Occasionally, the speech irregularity or slow developing vocabulary are obviously housed in a little boy with a deeper than normal voice. In such cases the low voice is likely related to the strength of the androgen bath during fetal development. Boys, as a group, develop language more slowly than girls, have more speech and pronunciation problems, and are more vulnerable to stuttering, stammering, and other speech-interruption patterns. Right-brained, that is left-handed or left-eye-dominant, boys may be as fluent in language development as any girl, but their speech center was obviously switched to the right hemisphere and escaped unscathed when the androgen bathed the left hemisphere and corpus colossum.

TIGER IN HIS TANK

As a baby boy arrives in the world, already with an active punching record in utero, his testosterone and other androgens are likely to promote a continued higher activity level when compared to girls of the same age. Indeed, hyperactive may be a word applied far too widely, since boys normally need more space and options for physical activity than girls. Crowded classes at church or school are frequently the real culprit behind what Diane McGinness at Stanford University has noted as a conspiracy between mothers, teachers, and physicians to overprescribe medication for otherwise normal-activity-level boys.[4]

The young boy's hormonally fueled energy will link up by the onset of pubescence with his more explicit sexual energy. Unlike his sister, whose sexual development may be taken in stride as a rite of passage into adult fertility status, the boy is confronted with a very different task. He has management responsibility for external genitals which begin to present themselves with a demanding appetite for pleasure and release. There simply is no parallel pattern in a young woman wherein ovulation and menstruation drive her to satisfy the biological release of reproductive material through a pleasure event.

The sea of adolescent sexuality is difficult enough to navigate alone. But when young men or women are placed in a sexually seductive culture, they may become easy pawns for greedy adults who target them with product advertising, music, film, and television programs calculated to exploit their sexuality for corporate or private adult profits.

In my *Parents, Kids, and Sexual Integrity*, I offer families options for holding the cultural seduction at bay through the cultivation of significant family decisions and practices. For us here it is enough to understand that young males' biological makeup causes them to be extremely vulnerable to sexual seduction. On one hand, their sexual energy is packaged so that daily fertility production is wrapped in enormous potential for pleasure, and on the other, they are intuitively aware that they are made for one exclusive, lifelong relationship. Too often, the time between first ejaculation and probable marriage seems to span at least half an eternity. It is into this "adolescent crucible" that young men move. During this period there will be enormous tests of will and integrity. And most young men will feel that they have failed either through masturbation, sexual contact with other males, or through premature genital contact with females.

If anthropologist J.D. Unwin's striking findings among eighty worldwide stone age cultures apply, as he thinks they do, to all human cultures, we are in big trouble with our "adolescent vacuum." In that vacuum both our young men and our young women are suspended between the world of innocent childhood and productive adulthood. I grieve across several chapters in *Parents, Kids, and Sexual Integrity* about our exploitation of our young—our nonrenewable human resources! There I describe the "adolescent crucible" and offer hope for standing with our kids as they bite the bullet of their desire for autonomy, productivity, and intimacy and obey our cultural lock-out signals. But we must also stand alongside those who capitulate and are devastated by their misadventures in autonomy, productivity, and intimacy. Healing and hope for their recovery will have to be everybody's business. I hold the culture in contempt for the deliberate exploitation of our young: the offers of a fantasy world of (1) freedom *without* responsibility, (2) extravagant display of goods without the opportunity to work and to produce significant income, and (3) sexual pleasure without commitment, responsibility, and exclusive fidelity.

Unwin reports, quite against his early forecast, that: there is an absolute "cause-effect" correlation between cultural creativity, productivity, and expansiveness *and* pre-marital abstinence, post-marital monogamous fidelity, and a sense of religious awe. This is visible in the erection of shrines with roofs and entrances by which people can walk in full upright postures—denoting a sense of the Transcendent. There is every reason to suspect that Unwin's cultural findings show up in individual instances, especially among men where sexual energy is such a dominant force.[5]

As we look at men's unfinished business, their sexuality constitutes the major moral curriculum. If they are to become honest and vulnerable men, capable of intimacy and gentleness as husbands and fathers, they will have to pass the integrity test regarding their sexuality. To become productive men in their careers, with vision and single-mindedness in pursuit of goals, they will have to find ways of harnessing their gigantic "tiger in the tank." The choices are an exclusive monogamous marriage or absolute celibacy. Whatever the choice, they will still be responsible for channeling the exploding sexual energy of their young manhood with integrity. For those who find themselves without a vibrant marital partner with whom to build exclusive intimacy, integrity calls them to excellence by joining the ranks of the honest and abstinent heroes. Their sexual energy will drive ambition, productivity, creativity, and what Unwin calls "expansiveness"—the vision to explore, bring into captivity, and develop new frontiers of intelligence, service, and space.

TWO

◇

THE SPITTING IMAGE OF HIS FATHER

While teaching at Princeton, Robbie and I were the guests of Dan and Jan Johnson one evening. The highlight of our time together was watching their young son, Derin, at play. Derin, then about five years old, gave us a demonstration of his pre-Little League skills. His athletic endowments, even at that young age, were already visible. But as Dan pitched a dozen balls so we could watch the eye-hand coordination of young Derin's batting, we noticed that before each ball was released, Derin tucked his head forward over his left shoulder and released a tiny fleck of spit. Only then could he flex into position to assess the coming ball.

Back inside the house, I asked Dan about Derin's spitting ritual.

"I'm afraid he came by that honestly. It is something I do, and he watches all of the church-league games. I'm sure he thinks it is the essential trademark of being a Johnson at the plate."

In a recent semester I announced to each of my four

spiritual formation groups, consisting of about ten men each, that we would spend the next three months drawing on stories about our relationships with our fathers. Reading the *Chicago Tribune* story of Ken Druck's "Alive and Male" seminars, I decided to open the father subject with my forty men. On the opening day, I selected an anecdote centered on my relationship with my dad during junior high. The agenda set off shock waves inside a couple of the participants. They made immediate appointments and came to see me privately. Dale said, "This is scary. Before it's time for me to talk about my father, I need to try expressing some of the things to you alone." Will reported, "My wife has been telling me that my bad temper with her is rooted in my anger and resentment toward my father. Can we talk about it privately before I open this up with the group?"

I have found that men can tell the deep truth best in a support network which has an open agenda of truth-telling and confidentiality. Without that, many men wither and hide their deepest questions and fears. Others seek out the confidentiality of male, often macho, adventures which have gestures of unbridled and uncensored speech but tend to fall short of actual baring of their souls. But in a lightly structured men's group dedicated to health and wholeness, they can plumb the deepest subjects. They can embrace and revive stifled feelings locked inside when mutual respect and full participation in a common agenda create the necessary confidential setting.

Men with a damaged father connection will be healed only to the extent that they can describe the loss and the pain. A support network group is the best environment for this. It is often superior to seeing a private therapist, primarily because the healing accelerates with a wide emotional support base. Another support group advantage is that every story tends to trigger parallel experiences in the other participants. Instead of feeling isolated, each truth-teller discovers that his individual pilgrimage is enriched and mirrored by this band of fellow pilgrims.

Children with damaged or lost relationships with either parent have a strong instinctual tendency to establish a surrogate connection. Sometimes it is found in a neighbor. That was Dale's case: "My father was home, but he had no time for me and showed no affirmation or affection for me. I actually was raised by the guy across the street. He had a son my age, and I guess it wasn't too much trouble for him to do everything with two of us instead of his son alone. That neighbor today remains my model of manhood and fathering."

Father loss, whether by death, abandonment, desertion, or divorce evokes a deep grief. Yet sometimes grief is short-circuited or choked, and remains in the denial stage. Gerry found himself simultaneously enrolled in a course on "death and dying," and in my Discipleship Development in the Family, where we opened the windows on childhood disruptions that are common in families, including "father absence." Here he was, a fully developed adult, put in touch with a grief that was buried back at age seven. Within a few weeks, he was able to link that loss to a small cluster of baffling fears and negative compulsions. A support network of trusted peers can bear the burden of grief shared at any stage or season of life.

Dan, abused by an alcoholic father, then rejected by a stepfather, despaired of being able to be a decent father to his own children. He had wandered through his college and seminary years largely as a loner. I found this treasure of a young man in a summer camping course, where he displayed absolute magic in working with troubled teenage boys. As his story began to surface, I invited him into a support network group where his scarred past continues to be healed.

Unlike Dan, most children reach out to replace a missing or a dysfunctional father. The church, school, and community environments tend to offer candidates for this reverse adoption. If we understood better how to be surrogate parents we might recognize a child's reaching out signals better. Accordingly, we would staff our agencies and classrooms more intentionally with magnetic and available adults. Ideally, we would train volunteers and employees in day-care centers, schools, and church agencies—equipping them to identify and provide potential surrogate fathers for those growing numbers of children whose homes are father absent.

FATHERS AS FATHER
Both our culture and our genes combine to give us a sense that our fathers make and control our destinies. In patrilinear cultures, the family name, identity, and property pass from fathers to children. Sometimes it is inherited by sons alone, especially in those cultures which sell daughters for a bride price.

David McKenna, president of Asbury Theological Seminary, unpacked the "father connection" for me in doing a biblical exposition of Mark 1:11. His address at the 1983 annual campus Ministers' Conference was entitled, "Jesus' Credentials for Ministry: Affirmed by God." In that address, he illuminated with his own story the words of God the Father delivered through an angel as Jesus came out of the water at His baptism, "This is My Son, whom I love; with Him I am well pleased" (Matt. 3:17).

McKenna asserted that God's affirmations were sweeping:

> I claim you. I love you. I am proud of you. Everyone needs to belong, to be loved, to be praised. When God says "I claim You," Jesus finds the strength of His identity. When God says, "I love You," He finds the strength of His security. And when God says, "I'm proud of You!" He has His sense of worth. This is the unshakable identity that Jesus took as His credential into His public ministry. We too

need these strengths of personhood. These are the relational credentials we must have if our ministry is to be effective: a sense of identity, of security, and a sense of self-worth.

To drive home the importance of these words from the Father to the Son, McKenna put hundreds of clergy into a breathless trance by noting the probability that in such a gathering there would be people stung by abandonment and by the terror of divorce.

Then he confided, "I personally know a bit of that hurt and I can speak about it because I can feel those wounds." He unfolded the story of his father's announcement to him at a drive-in restaurant that he was leaving his mother for another woman. "Then digging deeper, he told me that he had married my mother only to give me a name. A bond was cut for the next fifteen years between us." McKenna reports that the bond was repaired in a final reconciliation when he was able to say, "I love you!" just before his father died.

McKenna went on, "Perhaps that is why my proudest moments are when I introduce my children. I love to say 'This is my son!' or 'This is my daughter!' I want the whole world to know that I love them, that they are mine, and that I am proud of them. We belong to each other!"

The loss of a father, devastating as it is for both sons and daughters, tends to do the greatest violence to males. They typically are assigned, or abandoned, to remain with the mother. Thomas Parish's findings about the dynamics of divorce demonstrate a pattern few of us would have guessed. If the mother's fortunes improve after the divorce, the boy's sense of self-worth diminishes. If she enjoys fewer comforts and life gets tougher, the boy's self-worth rises. Evidently sons are so attached to their fathers' identities and sex roles that they are watching a subtle "stock market" to see whether males have any real value.[1]

If any blockage settles down between a father and a son, whether by divorce or abandonment, the son very often sets out to prove his own worth in the eyes of his absent father. Some of the highest motivation ever studied is in these driven men.

Mack appealed to me during his college freshman year. He was baffled by a messy expulsion he had survived when his father had put an ultimatum to him the day the divorce was final: "You decide whether you want to be with me or your mother. If you choose her, I will never speak to you again. You will no longer be my son. Mack and his sister, Melody, chose to stay with their father. A younger brother went with their mother. The expulsion came during the summer after Mack had graduated from high school. His father found him talking on the phone long distance to his mother. "I'll give you twenty-four hours to be out of here." So Mack packed suitcases, a few boxes, and a gigantic trunk and was off for his mother's place until college. I met him only a few weeks after he had entered college.

Five years later, with a mounting log of rejection of his efforts to write, phone, and send Christmas gifts and seasonal greetings to his father, Mack unveiled the anguish to the brown-bag lunch support group. Across the years, Mack had meticulously organized his life. And his aspirations were well above "mere survival." He worked for his own support, persistently pulled down top grades, ran for campus office, and carried on a "high-fidelity" weekend ministry. Mack also courted and married. Now with a baby just arrived, he was exploding. He told us why.

"Eileen's family is so supportive. And my mom and her husband are easy to deal with. But we decided that when the baby was born we would notify all three households, even though my dad has not spoken to me, written, or phoned since he put me out five years ago. So we made up three slips of paper with their names on them, to see who we would call first. Dad's name came up first. I have never even seen the woman he married after I left home. But I called. Dad answered the phone. I said, 'Congratulations! You are a grandfather for the first time!' I heard the click and the dial tone and thought I would die. But I turned to face the window so Elieen couldn't see my face, and I manufactured a one-sided conversation—a short one—to mask the rudeness of his rejection one more time."

Emotional abandonment can occur with the victim remaining under the same roof. Sons' unfinished business with their fathers often centers around feelings that they are worthless—as proved by their fathers' rejection. When parents divorce, it is common that adult sons and daughters are devastated. The entire legal basis for their conception has collapsed, so they have, they often feel, entered into a new domain of emotional illegitimacy—surviving "out of wedlock."

"My Dad was my best friend until I was twelve years old," Bill told the whole class. "He taught me how to do everything around the place, plus fishing, overhauling motors—everything. But when I was about twelve years old he abandoned me—he pulled away. it was like I frightened him or something. So I was vulnerable to the whole scene of the city—the sex, drugs, and alcohol that were everywhere. He didn't help me deal with any of them and he knew I was a sitting duck for all that stuff."

Fathers with unfinished business of their own often shut down. Some are simply ignorant; no one ever took them into maturity as responsible men either. Others became entangled with compulsive alcohol, drugs, sex, or other addictions. A growing boy on the premises is a reminder of the father's lost years, and that can shut down the comradeship that was present during childhood. And for still other fathers, the son's emerging manhood quickens the flesh of the lost youth of the father, and the father moves into the fast track of a mid-life adventure into sexual infidelity, even promiscuity. The silence which follows is the visible mask for the father's guilt and shame. King David's adultery and murder involving Bathsheba came, significantly, as his young sons were entering their manhood. The father's adultery in that famous case was the obvious trigger for wave after wave of seduction, incest, rape, and more murder.

There is little doubt that unfinished business with fathers is men's number one agenda. To be a boy is to aspire to grow up to be a father. The idolatry flows inevitably between a son and his dad.

DISPOSABLE FATHER?

Yet fathers, with all of that clout and power in the family structure, are virtually powerless to maintain contact with a wife or a family if the mother chooses to abolish his role and relationship. Courts in the Western world consistently award children to the custody of mothers. Men may provide sperm for birth and money for sustenance, but they are easily cut out of the lives of their children. Listen to the worst possible case as George Gilder describes the role of the male in his *Men and Marriage*, "Although the man is needed in intercourse, artificial insemination has already been used in hundreds of thousands of cases. Otherwise, the man is altogether unnecessary. It is the woman who conceives, bears, and suckles the child."[2]

In this updated edition of his earlier *Sexual Suicides*, Gilder spins a theory by which he sees men, historically, as sexually inferior to women. Whereas a woman's sexuality drives her total life, men tend only to be marginally and occasionally sexual, their sexual appetite having little to do with most of their day by day work and survival. In this sense, Gilder suggests, mothering is a global and total task compared to fathering, which is more occasional and episodic. Men, Gilder says, are made "equal" by social conventions. He thinks it is not surprising that men have taken a firm grasp on the legal domain, at least partly to control and to protect this fragile role that men have when they are reduced to fertilization services alone.

He suggests it is men's strength, unequaled by the average woman, and men's ability to win food or money in the marketplace with which males have made a deal with women. In exchange for her comfort, care, and intimacy, he can promise to honor, protect, and provide for her and their children.

Gilder's social-biological theory is chilling, but it underscores the vulnerability of males. They may be exiled out of intimacy, marriage, and family at the whim or legal maneuvering of a woman. Their dominance is plausibly rooted in this insecurity, so women suffer from male violence and insensitivity as a male strategy to maintain control from their intrinsically weaker position. Relationships, especially marriages, which are plagued by these dynamics put both men and women in no-win situations.

FATHERS OMNIPOTENT

My daddy is bigger than your daddy! The childhood taunt focuses on the "super-person" in a little boy's world. Fathers earn their domain, at least in the little boy's eyes. Who can free stuck windows, open well-seasoned jars of canned fruit, or untangle impossibly confused fishing line? Daddy, of course. To whom does Mom and the whole family turn when the going gets tough? Wait, of course, until Daddy gets home, and he will fix it.

So, accustomed as men are to indulging in this microcosm of omnipotence, they tend to wade fearlessly in on any problem assuming that they, indeed, can fix it. There is a curious and almost exclusively male impulse to fix things. Men tend to assume whenever a problem or pain arises that they are expected to fix it. They are typically more interested in fixing things than asking questions, listening, sympathizing, or grieving with people who want to relate to them.

This male omnipotence tendency is grounded in the fact that male musculature accounts for 42 percent of the adult body, compared to about 20 percent musculature in an adult female's weight. Males are equipped to make a major contribution through their strength, prowess, and protection. But when such display of male strength is deformed, motivated by insecurity, or marshalled to mask feelings of inferiority, it can become abusive, cocky, or violent to destructive extremes.

FATHERS OMNISCIENT
The same insecurity that may drive a father or any male to dominate, to assume that they are responsible for fixing everything, drives dogmatism—the closed mind. The husband of a woman who looks to him for all wisdom, either out of reverence and respect, or out of laziness and the luxury of being a "kept woman," will easily fall into the trap of becoming the omniscient, all wise decision maker.

Conservative religious traditions tend to exalt male omniscience: Isn't the man supposed to be the head of the house? is a common question among them. Both women and men ask the question. Yet the Scriptures nowhere speak of male "headship" to suggest that men omnisciently rule or have dominion over women. St. Paul advises children to "Obey your parents in the Lord, for this is right" (Eph. 6:1), but no passage of Scripture calls for *obedience* of wives to husbands or husbands to wives. Translators have to repeat the verb in Ephesians 5:22, "Wives *submit* to your husbands..." to make it demand unilateral submission of women to men. Verses 21 and 22 should actually read, "Submit yourselves to one another out of reverence for Christ. Wives, to your husbands as to the Lord." The italicized "submit" in 5:22 of the *New American Standard Version* does not serve the normal role of emphasis. Instead, it is the translators' way of telling us that it was added by recent human decision. And when you consider that the *New*

International Version translators also separate the passages by placing 5:22 under a new subhead, it is reasonable to question the motives of editors who would dare divide a submission concept that God joined together. This is all the more so when they knowingly reinforce a heresy by breaking the passage in the wrong place. Paul's use of "head" is consistently *cephale,* or a literal anatomic head which is useless and dead unless it is connected to a healthy body. So the Ephesian's material holds up both Eden's "two become one" and also offers the new "head and body" image of a whole person who is healthy, in unity, and able to accomplish tasks with the full energy of head and body synchronized. The opposite—a "chain-of-command marriage—would suggest a power control and even an adversary position. Marriage then would look spastic, and when Jesus is separated from the church, His body, by neurological damage, we have a spastic church.

Notice how Ephesians 5:21-33 appears in the *New International Version:*

²¹Submit to one another out of reverence for Christ.

Wives and Husbands

²²Wives, *submit* to your husbands as to the Lord. ²³For the husband is the head of the wife as Christ is the head of the church, his body, of which he is the Savior. ²⁴Now as the church submits to Christ, so also wives should submit to their husbands in everything.

²⁵Husbands, love your wives, just as Christ loved the church and gave himself up for her ²⁶to make her holy, cleansing her by the washing with water through the word, ²⁷and to present her to himself as a radiant church, without stain or wrinkle or any other blemish, but holy and blameless. ²⁸In this

same way, husbands ought to love their wives as their own bodies. He who loves his wife loves himself. [29]After all, no one ever hated his own body, but he feeds and cares for it, just as Christ does the church—[30]for we are members of His body. [31]"For this reason a man will leave his father and mother and be united to his wife, and the two will become one flesh." [32]This is a profound mystery—but I am talking about Christ and the church. [33]However, each one of you also must love his wife as he loves himself, and the wife must respect her husband.

Notice that the translators here and in other versions have arbitrarily inserted a "side heading" splitting the text even though the verb "submit" appears only in verse 21 and must set the stage for women (in verse 22) and for men in suggesting the tenderness of their love in verse 25—in the servanthood/submission mode. I have italicized the word "submit" which the *New American Standard Version* honestly reports is not in older and better manuscripts.

Only the doctrine of the Fall, as recorded in Genesis, names a top power position for the man. "He will rule over you" (Gen. 3:16) is not God's order for marriage or the family. It is a curse and a consequence of the Fall, not God's norm for relationships. We should repent of and resist this negative pull of sin instead of baptizing the urge to dominate and calling it "the Christian marriage." The idea of "head" denotes a fragile but indispensable contribution which a man makes to the "total person," of which the wife is the "body." The total person requires absolute health and synchrony between head and body, between the man and the woman. What a pity it would be to have a spastic marriage, a head and body uncoordinated through consensus. The Creation gift of dominion was to "them" (Gen. 1:28). The dominion mandate over creation is in the immediate context of God creating them male and female in His image.

Male omniscience is a heavy mantle to wear, and it assigns or accepts responsibilities no human can execute satisfactorily. Some men may come close to perfection, but the lone-ranger-executive male frequently carries the wounds of his wrongly accepted domain: hypertension and heart disease.

Since men are physically endowed to be primitive breadwinners and muscle-based providers, they once tended to dominate exclusively in a world where knowledge and wisdom were essential for survival. It is easy to see that the hunter, warrior, gatherer male might be looked to by women and children as the wizard of the wild world. But today, things are different—women as well as men work widely and have communication access to the entire global village. Still, in many families, the myth of the omniscient male remains virtually unchallenged, however myopic it may be.

A young man growing up today is exposed to powerful but contradictory messages about what is intrinsically masculine. The exaggerated omnipotence-omniscience model remains in many religious communities, but it also shows up in the survivalist and cultic camps which practice racism and elitism. Unfortunately, the more flexible biblical vision of man and woman in union forming the whole person is often lumped with a radical feminism which demands an end to male dominance and seeks to create a woman's world where men are reduced to indentured sperm bank depositors. This misunderstanding fails to take into account the distinct differences between the biblical pattern for relationships and the presuppositions of the radical feminists.

FATHER'S JUSTICE

Listen to one boy's veneration of Father: "When the teacher flunked all of the boys on a Spanish test and gave all of the girls A's, I was really angry. I knew if I told my dad, he would fix that teacher good."

Mothers come to their children's defense, of course.

But for some reason men seem to be endowed with a sense of fairness and justice existing apart from feelings or careful prediction of the consequences. Males are likely to act reflexively to "make things right"; perhaps it is their brawn. More likely it is rooted in their brain organization, which more clearly separates logic from feelings. So objectivity in justice comes naturally for males. Women's justice tends to weigh the human consequences of decisive action and delay judgment for fear of inflicting pain, rather than striking quickly to make things right.

This sense of justice which seems instinctual in young, ripening males is likely the "righteousness" dimension of the image of God—invested at Creation when the *imago dei* was distributed to male and female. Looking at the gift of "encompassing attachment" which is profoundly and generously planted in healthy females, we may be staring into the face of the other side of God's image. Woman can provide the magnetic balancing of God's loving-kindness or steadfast love over against the impartial righteousness and justice of man.

UNFINISHED BUSINESS WITH FATHER

In Arthur Miller's play, *Death of a Salesman*, Willy Loman is the idol of his wife, Linda, and the rising star of his two sons, Happy and Biff. They imagine that he is the most successful salesman in the world and that when he dies famous people will grieve his death.

This ideal father image is put in the fiercest artistic spotlight when Biff misses graduating from high school by four points lost on his math final exam. Willy is selling in Boston, so Biff hitchhikes there to find the hotel where his father always stays. He finds the room but has a hard time getting Willy to answer the door. After carefully hiding a prostitute in the bathroom, Willy finally faces Biff at the door. But when Biff cracks a joke, she laughs, and the secret is revealed. Biff's vision of Willy is immediately shattered. Willy takes over, he violently demands that Biff and he go home to get those points Biff needs to graduate.

Biff, realizing Willy is a charlatan, explodes, "He [the math teacher] would never listen to you. . . . You fake, you phony little fake! You fake!"

Years later, a perplexed Willy asks longtime neighbor Bernie whatever happened to Biff. "It's like something hit him like a hammer, and he laid down and died! He never accomplished anything after he flunked math." But Bernie's response angers Willy. He pointedly recalls the time that Biff literally gave up on life. He then asks Willy Loman the most penetrating question of the entire drama, "What happened up in Boston when Biff went looking for you?"[3]

Boys need their father's blessing and their fidelity to the naive ideal of childhood idolatry. But any form of dishonesty between father and son sets an agenda of "unfinished business" that frequently haunts the adult life of the son, often damaging his aspirations, marriage, and parenting behavior.

Jeff's story is a mirror of such behavior: "I can't believe how messed up my dad is. I have two older sisters, and he has made life miserable for all three of us. My mom sees what he is doing to us. I called home over last weekend, for example, and he started up this big fight. So when I finally hung up at the end, I just felt terrible, like 'What's the use of living, if I'm as worthless as he says?'"

Jeff was a handsome young man, single, and in the prime of young life—just under twenty-five. I had never seen him before, and my sign-up sheet was filled when he really needed to talk the week before. But here he was in my office now, with a lifelong load of questions. I asked how his father treated people outside of the family.

He responded, "Wonderfully. In fact, he is very popular in our home community. He teaches physical education, and the students all love him. I have watched him deal with his gym class kids and with regular class-room students. He treats them like royalty—really gracious and affirming with them. But something happens when he gets home; he treats us all unbelievably shabbily."

"How does he treat your mom?"

"Like she was his mother or something—no magne-tism that I've ever seen. He cares *about* her, but not *for* her, I think. And he's rude to her sometimes, but it's like he knows he better not bite very hard the hand that feeds him."

"And how does he treat you and your sisters?"

"My sisters are married, so the relationship has changed. Dad is basically your decent, civil person. He shows off well in public, and dishes out the money when we need it."

"Is he picking up the tab on your tuition and living expenses now?" I inquired.

"No. My mom works and she's helping me. I'm sure none of his money goes to pay any of my bills. When I'm home, though, he will pull out his wallet when I am leaving and hand me a twenty or a couple of them."

"Is your dad available at important times? Is he pre-dictably there," I asked Jeff, "or does he have a habit of missing the important things in your life? Will he come to your graduation here, for example?"

"He'll be here, and everybody will think he's a won-derful guy. When he was at my ball games, for example, he was really cool. My friends thought I was really lucky to have a dad like that. It was when I got home that he lit into me, always criticizing and humiliating me in front of the family. He called me awful names—unbelievable and despicable ones. I was really confused by that, be-cause he seemed to like me when I was with my friends. I'm thankful for that. He didn't embarrass me in front of my friends. But sometimes I think I must be losing my mind, to have had such terrible experiences with this man behind closed doors at home."

"Tell me about your mom," I continued with Jeff.

"How does she deal with your dad?"

"She manages very well. And she tells us she is sorry that we don't see Dad at his best, that really he is a very good person. We are right, she says, to be angry at the way he is putting us down all the time, and she wishes we would stand up to him some way.

"I remember she has often told me in one way or another, 'Don't grow up to be like your daddy.' That has been the hardest thing to handle. There is so much about him that I admire, but at home he's a jerk. So I've been close to my mother. She says she has tried to tell him how he has mistreated us by ruthlessly criticizing and humiliating us."

Biff in *Death of a Salesman* and Jeff carry symptoms of what Dan Kiley calls *the Peter Pan Syndrome*.[4] The most visible symptom is their social paralysis. These Peter Pans seem unable to enter into full adult male responsibility—a subtle point made in the Peter Pan musical where the part requires a young woman to play the Peter role, in an effort to show a "boy" with unchanged voice and childhood preoccupations. These "Peter Pan" adult men suffer from shattered self-respect, insecurity from watching an unpredictable father, and feelings of having been betrayed by him. All of this has damaged the sense of self.

Whether we think of that damage as being to the "inner child of the past," or the "figurine within," or as a "hole in the soul," the painful imagery tells it all. The damage is early and deep, and is the root of symptoms he will bear in the adolescent and adult years. Most of these disappointing fathers were themselves damaged in their childhood. At some level the wounded sons and the damaged fathers are both victims. But we can trace this "unfinished business" with fathers, typically, across four or five generations before the dramatic effects begin to fade. Exodus 20:4-6 states the taboo against "idolatry," and follows with an explanation about the "Peter Pan" effect: "You shall not make for yourself an idol in the form of anything in heaven above or on the earth beneath or in the waters below. For I, the Lord your God, am a jealous God, punishing the children for the sin of the fathers to the third and fourth generation of those who hate me, but showing love to a thousand generations of those who love me and keep my commandments." Are we describing "idolatries" of confused priorities or hidden "gods" who control fathers? And do these priorities constitute "hating" God by ignoring the father tasks and the path of repentance that would bring wholeness in a single generation to stop the chain-effect devastation from father to son to grandson?

SONS OF THEIR FATHERS

Watch any young boy imitate Dad talking or walking, and you get a clue into the powerful imprint fathers make on their sons. To be a boy is to be in the image of Daddy, to want more than anything else to grow up to be like Dad.

The carbon copy gestures, speech, and actions of sons compared to their fathers is strong enough to feed the old nurture versus nature debate and to settle it on the nurture side entirely. But what is terrifying is the tendency of boys to mimic the violent or irresponsible male behaviors equally well.

Harry Chapin's *The Cat's in the Cradle*, a haunting parable of son imitating father says it all: "I'm going to be like you, Dad. You know I'm gonna be like you." The son's words turn into a self-fulfilling prophecy. In the song, the father who had no time for the little boy or the teen, eventually discovers that he is old and his son can't find time for him either.

The boy has turned out just like his father. When a father habitually neglects, criticizes, or rejects a son, a powerful and destructive message is turned loose. Adult children of alcoholics, for example, are a group who have to deal with the lifelong devastating effects of damage to the core of personality. It is evidenced in the area of self-respect. If that respect was not filled up by a consistent, affirming, and fair father, it will take a network of friends in the adult years to fill the damaged cup of self-respect. The cup is not only empty, but it has developed a "hole" which prevents the affirmation of others from beginning to fill it. Daddy's negative evaluation outweighs them all.

It is not surprising that Kenneth Druck reports from his *Alive and Male* seminars that men's unfinished business with their fathers is the most persistently recurring emotional block in their lives. Druck reports that the men in his seminars were eager to talk about their fathers. He discovered that while most men carry vestiges of an unresolved past, they needed someone else to prime them for a reconciliation. Thus, his seminar thrives with its primary focus on men's unfinished business with their fathers.[5]

For example, if men are unable to express feelings to their wives, the roots seem to be in the father connection. If they can acknowledge and verbalize deep feelings about their fathers, their emotions revive and they reenter the human race as changed men.

Evangelist Bill Glass, speaking to a businessmen's luncheon in Fort Wayne, Indiana, told of his visits behind bars. Glass has been admitted to more prisons than any other guest speaker. He asserted that he has not met one man in prison who has feelings of respect or affection for his father. Instead, feelings of hatred, resentment, and indifference express the full range of feelings toward their fathers.

In *Bonding: Relationships in the Image of God,* I report the key question I use when anyone expresses a fading belief in God: Tell me about your relationship with your father. Indeed, it was that question which triggered Jeff, whose story I mentioned earlier and will again in chapters 6 and 7. His first appointment was one made to open the subject of his unbelief and inability to find meaning in prayer.

Except for intentional seminars and the rare support groups a few men cultivate, many get in touch with their feelings through the mask of alcohol or street drugs. Men can talk about painful agendas over beer. They can even embrace each other in the bar. If they break through the boundaries of social propriety in talking or touching, they can always disclaim the event: "I was a little drunk." Unfortunately, the anesthesia strategy of using alcohol to mask the intimate truth-telling lets men down when they are sober. Then they are only humiliated and ashamed in new ways. They find themselves having to return to a reality which demands that they deny the feelings they expressed when they were out of control.

This book is my report on men's hunger for honesty, integrity, and intimate truth-telling. I am reporting in detail how lightly structured but intentional support networks are a magnet for men who want to be fully whole, fully alive, and fully male. Chapter 11 will suggest a series of light-agenda starters for men's support or spiritual formation groups.

Every man longs to be connected to an ideal father. That is tremendously good news. Boys keep an eye on the high school teacher, youth minister, or professional athlete. The secret behind this search is likely this, God has invested one version of His image in the human male. There is only one perfect Father, and all of us who are human fathers are only "images," however flawed and imperfect, of the One who has no peer.

THREE
◇

HIS MOTHER'S BOY

One of the most remarkable women I ever met was Julia Shelhamer. She was a legend by the time I was fifteen, when I read her husband's amazing book *Heart Talks for Boys*. Julia's name appeared on the companion volume, *Heart Talks for Girls*. I first met Julia when she moved to Winona Lake, Indiana. She would have been in her eighties. Later, our family moved to Wilmore, Kentucky, where she had moved to spend her final years with her daughter and son-in-law. And I was on hand when, on her 100th birthday, she asked Dr. J.C. McPheeters, Asbury's second president, himself in his nineties, to pray for her and commission her as she began her second century in ministry.

Julia was a veteran of street rescue mission operations in Shreveport, Louisiana and Washington, D.C. So when she first arrived at Winona Lake, Indiana, she was out of her elements. Dr. J.F. Gregory, then editor of his denomination's magazine, *The Free Methodist*, asked her soon after her arrival, "How do you like Winona Lake?"

Julia's instant reply shocked him, "Very well, but I miss the drunks." So Julia embarked on a career of visiting bars and cocktail lounges on Thursday afternoons. I asked her once, since my wildest imagination could not picture this godly little old woman in a bar, "What do you do when you visit the cocktail lounges and bars?"

"Oh, Mr. Joy," she said, "you know that three of us older women go every Thursday afternoon. But younger women couldn't do what we do. I always ask the proprietor whether I can speak to his patrons, of course. And I have never been refused. Then I approach some man who is sitting all alone, and I sit down near him. When he looks at me, I say to him, 'Do you have a mother?' "

"Tell me about your mother," opens one of the most important windows into any person's life. And it may be that sons are more attached to their mothers than daughters are. I have asked myself this question when I see consistent signals in our culture of this special relationship: What is it that motivates NFL players to wave greetings to their mothers when the television cameras play on them? Are they men without fathers? Or is there a special linkage between a young man and his mother?

In *Bonding: Relationships in the Image of God*, I speculate about the curious breaking away rituals which girls practice to establish autonomy from their mothers. But even more visible, in the standard two-parent family, are boys turning to their mothers as they launch into manhood. At that same time they become relatively distant to their fathers, as if to enter into the adult domain by themselves.

MOTHERS' GIFT
The bond between a natural mother and her child is unique, of course. The universal bonding principle that motivates mothers of all warm-blooded species to give constant and effective care and protection to the newly born or hatched is a miracle. Without it the infant mortality rate would quickly wipe out most species.

His Mother's Boy

We know in humans, for example, that vaginally delivered babies are so stressed by travel through the birth canal that they literally arrive with a brain released chemical high which causes them to spend up to at least their first three hours wide awake. During these hours birth-bonding tends to cement them to the mother's visual image, unique odors, and voice. To the extent that fathers can be brought into the birth-bonding hours, the same bonds can be established between father and infant. Indeed, fathers who give that first care while the mother is recovering from an unusually troublesome delivery, often find that their children continue to run for their arms when they need special care or comfort. In such cases the mother may feel rejected by such a spontaneous and lifelong pattern of primary dependency on the male. But the pattern remains strong because it is rooted in the hours immediately following birth.

Mothers, compared to fathers, simply by their own preference and by the opportunities afforded them in most cultures, spend more time with young children. They tend to accumulate more hours of simple caregiving than do fathers. Mothers are the center of attachment for most of us. We depend on them to be there, to provide food, and to comfort us. Mothers know us in a literal and naked sense. To look into mother's face is to realize that there is no place to hide from her; she knows us from the beginning.

For nearly twenty years I have sent my graduate students to tell stories to children and to elicit moral judgments from them about ways to fix things that have gone wrong. We often add some abstract definitions questions after the stories. One of the more interesting sets of responses comes when an interviewer asks, "Do you think God is more like a father or more like a mother?" And since we are replicating moral reasoning in these anecdotal interviews we steel ourselves against correcting their answers. My students have found that boys under ten years old often say that God is more like a mother than a father. "Why do you think God is more like a mother?" has to be the next question. Look at the logic and the concrete reality of the explanations we typically get: "Because He takes care of you." "God won't let you go hungry." "You can always come back when you've run away. That's the way it is with your mother."

When mother is the natural mother, she is literally the source of life. The seed of the woman leaves its genetic marker across the generations in a way that father's seed does not. So while most of us carry our fathers' names, we also carry the genetic marker in our mitochondrial DNA, by which we can be linked across all of our generations to all of our mothers, even to the first Mother. All living humans, researchers now have discovered, are literally descended from one woman. Male sperm carries no such multigenerational marker.[1]

MOTHERS' WARMTH

The origin of life occurs within the body of the mother, so it is easy to trace the child's magnetic pull toward her as the center of warmth—literally the oven of primal life. Add to that the happy effects of intimate contact in the early hours of life, and it is easy to see that life's surest security is deposited with Mother!

The affectional center of a family tends to rest, also, in Mother. I am intrigued by the rich metaphors of the Creation narrative in Genesis. Among those pictures which are worth contemplating is that of the woman being built up from the parts of Adam drawn from the *pleura*, literally the thorasic cavity. We have traditionally thought of the woman as being formed from man's rib, but two errors creep into that idea.

1. Adam is clearly the complete humanity prior to sexual differentiation, as both woman [literally *Ishah*] and man [literally *Ish*] are formed from "Adam."

2. The word commonly translated "rib" is a construction term, not an anatomic word and refers to the vertical pieces of the interior of the hull of a wooden boat—

the ribs. So it is easy to expand the surgical imagery of Creation to see why the Hebrew *tsela* was translated *pleura* in the first Greek translation of the Old Testament. Both evoke images of the entire thorasic cavity opened, much as modern open-heart surgery separates the rib cage at the sternum and goes into the life center of our body.

The heart denotes the center of affections and beliefs in biblical imagery; the opening of the center of Adam was likely intended to give us a picture of mother as one created out of the most affectional resources present in Adam—the totally human being. Research has validated this point, for women taken as a group, consistently score higher than men on affective and affectional measures. Isabel Myers found, when she validated her now famous Myers-Briggs Personality Inventory, that sex differences appeared only in one pair of poles in her four sets: 60 percent of women compared to 40 percent of men showed a preference for making decisions based on "feeling," or the "human considerations" involved. Just the opposite pattern showed for "thinking," or "pure rational factual decision-making": men, 60 percent and women, 40 percent. On all other scales men and women were evenly divided.[2] Remember that women's brains combine both feelings and reasoning, while men are often "single minded."

With this sex difference, we see how sons might find this "opposite" characteristic in mother to be a powerful magnet. Placed between a rational father and an affectional mother guarantees a child will be aware of the full spectrum of environment in which he has been spawned. And the extent that opposites attract may be another reason why sons tend to depend on mothers.

The opposite magnet provides the clue to mothers' powerful attachment to their sons. Indeed, so desperate is the yearning of a young woman for male affirmation that one of the most pronounced effects of father absence for her shows up in the search for a man. This pilgrimage, which sets out to replace the missing father in her life, often leads her to premature sexual adventures and pregnancy. But the startling bottom line of her search consistently shows up in the research on father absence, in the illegitimate birthrate, and decisions to keep the baby. That bottom line consideration is reduced to a logical syllogism in the mind of a girl who feels abandoned by her father. It is simply this:

1. If I cannot have Daddy, I will find myself a man.
2. Any man will do, since I am so worthless and cannot ask for a really good catch.
3. If I get pregnant by a man, maybe he will marry me.
4. Even if he does not marry me, if I can have a baby, maybe it will be a boy. Then I will have a man at last.

In chapter 1 I summarized the profound difference between male and female brain organization. To the extent that a son suffers from that male single-mindedness, which tends to keep his affective right hemisphere from translating easily into the speech produced in his left hemisphere, it is likely Mother who best represents the boy's true feelings. Deprived of easy access in putting their feelings into words, boys may find it easier to ventilate those nonspeech expressions of emotions in Mother's presence. The tears, the sighs, and surrender of anger—all of these will be understood by Mother. Mother is the safe haven of affection, and no taboos exist in the Western world against a boy of any age who wants to hug his mother, hold her, or cry on her shoulder.

Daddy, in the eyes of the son, is more likely in his single-minded view of the world to either put logical solutions in place, give advice, or to simply ventilate emotions through symbols such as profanity. None of these reactions are particularly attractive to young boys, so it is to Mother's comfort that they flee.

MOTHERS' POLISH
Let me replay a scenario that is almost universal. Try to figure out what is going on.

His Mother's Boy

My son is going through my shaving gear in the master bathroom. I hear a shout, "Daddy! Can you come help me for a minute."

I go only to find that he has my electric razor out. He has already removed the darkening hair around his mouth and has squared off the teardrop sideburns that have been forming now for several weeks as the promise of real whiskers. All of that hair growth is gone. He has figured out the razor perfectly. After all, I had to give him a first turn at the age of two when he toddled in every morning during my shave, hoping that I would let him be a little man. After a few seconds of feeling the vibration of the back of the razor applied to his cheek, he was satisfied, his male sex role batteries charged for the day.

"Where is your shaving lotion—the kind you always use? I couldn't find it," he anxiously inquires.

I don't know how he missed that part of the secret male formula. No matter, I go into the lower section of the storage unit and retrieve the *Brut.* He takes over, and I leave him to apply my favorite scent. I offer him the facial talcum too, though I seldom bother to use it.

All is silent for a few minutes, then Mr. Handsome appears, ready for an important evening out. He looks like a million dollars, right down to his latest clothing, handpicked to his own taste. As he comes across the family room I notice an uneasy look on his face. I rise to praise him and see him off, but in his intensity, he charges right past me and into the kitchen.

"How do I look, Mom?" He is cautious with her—as if he is afraid of her response. His words are spoken softly as if they may be the last words he will ever speak, unless her response is one that will refuel his empty tank.

"Wow," she whispers. "I can't believe it, yet here it is: My son is a man. He is tall. He is handsome. And he even has the smell of a man on him. What ever happened to my baby boy?"

Imagine such a thing. Here I sit with the evening paper in my lap. I was good enough to provide the razor and to lay out the *Brut*. But who does he run to for an appraisal? His mother, some thanks! What does she know about manhood?

It would be easy to extend the scenario of self-pity and rejection, and to end up in an explosion of anger. If that happens, the father is marginalized, and the "mother-son" dyad becomes a competitive threat to the marriage. But the scene I have described is virtually never an expression of mother-son fixation or an alternative to marital attachment. Instead, the boy simply needs an authoritative judgment on his masculinity and marketability as a man, so he turns to the consumer professional—his mother.

Seen in this light, the boy's presentation to his mother is the highest compliment he can pay his father. It is as if the son is saying, Mom, look me over. Am I as well put together as Dad was when you first met him? Am I as good looking? Do I smell right? Do I pass your judgment? You were the one who picked Dad and I have imitated and admired him since I was born. Do I measure up?

Mothers do the "final polish" for sons, who growing up admiring their dads, have imitated every small detail of gender-appropriate behavior, right down to vocabulary and manner of walking. Dads furnish the same mirror for their daughters. Healthy teen and young adult women have fathers who admire and affirm them. Such women glow with a sense of wellness, defined by Daddy's words and the knowledge that he would die for their safety and well-being. In this way the image of God invested in the father-mother unit emerges again faithful to sons and daughters who need the final touch of affirmation to launch them as healthy women and men.

MOTHERS' LOVE
What is the core of personality? What are the core character components in men and women? At Harvard's

Center for the Study of Moral Development, Lawrence Kohlberg, in an important career cut short by his untimely death, reported exactly what Jean Piaget had found working with children in Switzerland: Justice is the core of human character, and it is universal across cultures. Justice, it turns out, begins with concern for the self, a cry for fairness. But as it unfolds in later childhood and into maturity, a healthy person applies the fairness rule to other people, eventually to all people, and a more complicated justice concern develops.

Kohlberg and Piaget worked almost exclusively with boys. Carol Gilligan, a Kohlberg student later turned colleague, courageously asked whether justice was indeed the core for women's moral judgments as well. For nearly twenty years, Dr. Gilligan has been giving us her findings. First in journal articles in the *Harvard Education Review*, and later in a book entitled *In a Different Voice*, she reported that females make moral judgments on a different foundation. That moral base is "attachment." Women become seriously involved in moral decisions. Their gift of feeling and reaching out to others is so enormous that they are unable to stand outside of a problem. Instead, they must solve problems while remaining intimately connected to all of the participants. Gilligan found the moral development of girls and women to parallel the unfolding justice structure in the classical research on boys and men, but female judgments are profoundly more subjective and complex than the calculating objective decisions of men.

This gift of attachment is an important balance to the more objective sense of justice which is required for minimum law and order in any human community. But the complementary balance of justice and love provides more than a self-correcting set of principles for society; the balance invested in dominant doses in children transforms individual and family life.

When we think of Mother's love, it is easy to become nostalgic and sentimental. Sweet as our memories might be, they fail to touch upon our real need. Humankind must bring Mother's love to bear not only in child-rearing and family relationships, but in the political arena at national and global levels.

The roots of Mother's attachment gift and of Father's justice perspective are most clearly traced in the doctrine of Creation. The "image of God" is distributed to and reflected in humanity as male and female. At its best, the sovereign, "wholly-otherness" of God's righteousness is imaged by the universal tendency of males to stand outside of events and make objective judgments. On the other hand, females image God's other side by embracing the world with unconditional love and attachment, and meting out judgments that take into account the subjective concerns of all participants.

At their worst, men make cold, insensitive judgments and become trapped victims of "the facts." Super-rational men, oblivious to the human dimensions of the world, knuckle under as workaholics, and serve as indentured slaves of things. And at their worst, women become emotionally attached to too many persons. They may be seduced into nearly fatal compromises, often unable to decide because the dilemmas are too complex. Such women often fall victim to mental overload, emotional paralysis, or psychological disorders. Their fatal cry is that of the first woman, "I was deceived."

It is clear that the "Mother Love" and "Father Justice" gifts are self-correcting where both are present, fully-charged, and attentive to each other. The nuclear family, then, is certainly the ideal environment in which to be formed as a healthy and balanced human.

MOTHERS' SUPERVISION
The mother-child attachment establishes the potential bond within which the child grows to responsible adulthood. Father-bonding, such as Joseph's providential role in Jesus' delivery, or as it is intentionally arranged in hospitals today, can provide parallel foundations for

high quality attachment between father and child from infancy throughout a lifetime.

There is no better predictor about children's "risk" for compulsive addiction to alcohol, sex, and drugs, than to look at their family system. I unfold four typical family systems in my *Parents, Kids, and Sexual Integrity*. A high quality father-mother relationship is the single best predictor of the healthy and risk-proof child.

One of the most intriguing family systems studies ever completed is rarely mentioned today. Yet the work of two Harvard Law School professors, published in 1950, under the title, *Unraveling Juvenile Delinquency*, was a comprehensive and carefully done study. Its accuracy for predicting households with potentially healthy or criminal boys is unrivaled. Today, we badly need a replication of the Sheldon and Eleanor Glueck study, both to bring it up to date and to extend it to the female population as well.

The Gluecks, weary of training law students whose energies would be consumed by large logs of adolescent criminal cases, set about to study the characteristics of delinquents—then almost exclusively boys. They were eager to unravel the causes of delinquency, in the hope that by knowing its sources, all of us could help prevent it. By "juvenile delinquency," the Gluecks referred to criminal convictions of juveniles, who, if they had been of legal age as adults, would have been prosecuted as a felony.

The Gluecks began by identifying 500 persistent delinquent boys and 500 nondelinquent boys who were matched by age, intelligence, ethnic derivation, and neighborhood conditions. The 1,000 boys were studied on more than 400 traits and factors. The researchers looked for anything which consistently correlated with delinquency or non-delinquency. From the 120 social factors in family backgrounds, 5 factors emerged which were found to accurately correlate with delinquency and non-delinquency—at opposite ends of the spectrums on

each of the 5 factors:
1. Discipline of the boy by the father
2. Discipline of the boy by the mother
3. Affection of the father for the boy
4. Affection of the mother for the boy
5. Cohesiveness of the family.

In 1952, the New York City Youth Board (NYCYB) began the first follow-up of young children to test the reliability of the Glueck social prediction table. They selected 303 boys, ages five and six, of white, black, Jewish, and Puerto Rican descent, and followed them for ten years. Since many of the boys came from mother only homes, Maude M. Craig and Selma J. Glick modified the Glueck five-point factors, reducing them to:
1. Discipline of boy by mother or mother substitute
2. Supervision of the boy by the mother
3. Cohesiveness of the family unit.

Craig and Glick developed some technical definitions, which we need to understand to proceed. "Suitable discipline" referred to parental correction that was reasonable and explained to the boy. It might include physical consequences, loss of privileges, and other common parent-child disciplines. The mother was consistent, verbal, and reasonable. "Unsuitable discipline" included none at all, along with inconsistent, unreasonable, punitive, and overly strict punishment for the slightest infraction of the mother's rules.

"Suitable supervision" included overprotection, and an agreement between mother and child that she must always know where the boy was and with whom he was associated. She needed to know his friends. If she worked outside the home, the boy must have been in the care of an adult who was equally committed to the boy's welfare. "Unsuitable supervision" included only partial knowledge about the boy, inconsistent attention to his welfare, and even emotional and physical abandonment.

"Cohesiveness in the family" was characterized by an atmosphere of affection and mutual dependence among family members. The boy found the home to be his important place of security and belongingness. Family celebrations were like clockwork, and meals brought the family together daily. The "unintegrated home," at the extreme delinquent end, was marked by the extreme self-interest of all family members—the house was a place to sleep. Meals were erratic and unpredictable, and virtually no attention was given to family celebrations.

Using those three factors and intermediate points in between the poles I have summarized here, the NYCYB across a ten-year span revisited the boys when they were fifteen and sixteen years old. They lost track of only 1 of the 303 boys in the sample. The results of the tracking for ten years was most astounding. Look at the reliability of the Glueck factors:

97.1 percent accuracy in predicting non-delinquency.

84.8 percent accuracy in predicting delinquency.[3]

Ken Magid, in his terrifying 1987 book, *High Risk*, reminds us that the lack of family bonding is presenting North America with such seriously damaged children that the entire culture is at risk. These potentially destructive, damaged children now coming in sizeable numbers into the adult population are an increasing worry. Given the economic reality of "two incomes" as the minimum basis on which to buy a home and launch a family, many parents may have put their children into the high risk pool of children we will fear. They will likely have made that decision by default, seeing their standard of living as more important than the stable environment they might have provided by investing fewer prime hours in the workplace. And the single parent, under so many stresses already, surely has a gigantic task in maintaining order and stability in the nontraditional household.

But the sign of peace and hope is clear: Mother's discipline, supervision, and structuring of family life, even for the single parent home, might leverage a 97.1 percent probability that the kids will not be adolescent criminals.

IN SEARCH OF MOTHER

We have no studies of mother absence to compare the likely effects on either sons or daughters. The father absence studies were begun following World War II, and established the effects on both sons and daughters. Eventually we found that those painful effects varied in predictable ways depending on other factors:

1. How early the loss occurred.
2. Why the father was removed from the world of the child.

Today, with the increasing cases of mother abandonment, and the significant number of single-parent homes headed by males, we deserve to know more clearly what those predictable mother absence effects might be. To inform our questions we might expect that children without mothers would suffer deprivation at obvious levels: affectional development, security, self-esteem, and confidence in their sex-role development.

Many years ago, now, I was intrigued with the central mother theme in Hermann Hesse's novel, *Narcissus and Goldmund*. In the story, young Goldmund is delivered to the monastic cloister by his father. When the senior priest reports to the faculty that the boy has no brothers or sisters, and no mother, he urges them to be a father to the boy to make up for his homesickness.

But Narcissus, a young teaching-monk, watches Goldmund flower from childhood into young manhood at eighteen. Narcissus reports to the Abbot that Goldmund suffers because he has forgotten a part of his past—his mother, and all connected with her.

The Abbot recalls that there may be a reason for the forgetting, and without telling Narcissus his thoughts, remembers that Goldmund's father had reported that his wife had abandoned them, run away when the boy was young, and brought shame upon them both. The father had tried to suppress the mother's memory in the boy. The Abbot speculated that he had succeeded, inasmuch as Goldmund gave up his life to God as an atonement for his mother's sins.

Without help from the Abbot, Narcissus eventually supports the depressed and failing Goldmund in his desire to leave the school and go in search of his own world. Most of the novel traces the playboy's search for love, his using and being used by women. Occasionally he returns to visit the cloister and to bring Narcissus up to date on his misadventures. After many years, Goldmund, fearfully ill and actually dying, returns to Narcissus. He has, by this time, established a fine reputation as a woodcarver who specializes in sanctuary images. His major unfinished piece is Eve—the original mother.

The closing days of Goldmund's life find him opening up the hidden memories of his mother. "Do you remember?" he asks Narcissus. "I had completely forgotten my mother until you conjured her up again." The powerful novel ends with Narcissus—the man who truly understood Goldmund, and who reads humanity as if it were an open book—receiving Goldmund's final confession.

"I cannot wait until tomorrow. I must say farewell to you now, and as we part I must tell you everything. Listen to me another moment. I wanted to tell you about my mother, and how she keeps her fingers clasped around my heart. . . ."

So Goldmund unfolds the summary of his quest and of his regret that the Eve figure is unfinished. "Only a short while ago it would have been unbearable to me to think that I might die without having carved her statue; my life would have seemed useless to me. And now see how strangely things have turned out: It is not my hands that shape and form her; it is her hands that shape and form me."

Having "studied" women for his entire adult life, he has been trying to portray all of womanhood and all of mother in his image of Eve.

Unfinished Business

"I can still see it, and if I had force in my hands, I could carve it. But she doesn't want that; she doesn't want me to make her secret visible," Goldmund explains.

Narcissus is deeply shaken by the confession and the revelation. Goldmund had known something about Narcissus that caught him off guard. Finally, the dying man opened his eyes, saying farewell without words. Then, suddenly, gathering all of his energy for a final question, he whispers, "But how will you die when your time comes, Narcissus, since you have no mother? Without a mother, one cannot love. Without a mother, one cannot die."[4]

Hesse's tale marks men well. Indeed, all men are born of women, and unfinished business between a man and his mother is at the root of much of the secret agony and unspeakable secrets hidden deep inside of men.

FOUR

TO BE HIMSELF

Ray obviously started out large for his age. Big-boned, tall, and lean as an adult, it was easy to believe his description of the early years.

"When I started to kindergarten the teacher took me aside and appealed to me to help her watch after this kid with severe problems. She had me figured out. Compliant child, wanting to please everybody, but especially adults, it was like they thought I was volunteering to be the teacher's helper. The same thing happened every year. I can name the kids I got assigned to. And I took it so seriously that I never did get to play or work with the ordinary kids. I was always 'baby-sitting' somebody with a big problem. I never complained."

Ray went on, "When I look at my class pictures from elementary school, I can see why they did it to me. I would have done it to myself. For example, in my second grade class picture I was as big as the teacher. There we stand. I am on the left end of the picture, and she is on the right end of the lineup. And in between the two of us are all of these normal little kids."

We were looking for the roots to Ray's adult loneliness and his lifetime of essentially being without people who were close to him. "When I hit seventh grade I discovered basketball. My dad had played basketball, so I knew it was a good option coming in junior high school. And I was good. I was so good that I got to play with older players, and performed competitively from seventh grade on. That gave me status, prestige, and recognition from my peers. But I didn't know how to relate to them any other way. It was very safe, socially, to earn my points in basketball competition; I didn't have to deal with real people. They would roar with applause; I was often their hero, but no relationships came with the applause. Off the court I wanted to hide. I simply didn't want to be around people. I felt clumsy and shy, yet I needed to be close to people."

It was clear. Ray's undeveloped social skills complicated the people dimension of his high school experience. And as an adolescent, as in other cases, there is a season for optimal development and general wholeness. In this chapter, I want to walk you through a time line I have discovered from working with men. It ranges across the full spectrum of emotional and spiritual health. Also, I want to identify basic needs and the timetable which seems to best serve that basic development toward wholeness.

BECOMING HUMAN: WELLNESS VS. WARP?

The first description of the human condition in the Judeo-Christian tradition is the Genesis 2:18 assertion, "It is not good that the human should be alone" (my translation). Isolated or growing up among animals, for example, a developing human being does not learn language. But put together, not alone but in community, we develop words as tools for dealing with others. Indeed, there is a curious rule that forms a baseline about relationships. During childhood, one needs daily contact with peers in direct proportion to the child's age. For example, if the child is four years old, he or she needs to spend four hours per day with peers. The only child, or the oldest child whose siblings do not arrive for several years, tends to develop with defective social skills. On the other hand, children of large families tend to have well-developed skills for dealing with conflict and a wide range of positive relationships.

Take a look at the time line. You will be able to sketch in your own critical experiences. I will prompt your thinking by describing some of the significant things that might be noted on the time line.

```
┌─────────────────────────────────────────────────────┐
│                                                       │
│        HUMAN DEVELOPMENT AND HEALTHY                  │
│               RELATIONSHIPS                           │
│                                                       │
│     World of                                          │
│     Experiences in                                    │
│     Loving                                            │
│   reLationships                                       │
│        N                                              │
│        E                                              │
│        S                                              │
│        S                                              │
│                                                       │
│   Birth   5   10   15   20   30   40   50   60   70   │
│                                                       │
│                           World of                    │
│                           Abnormal                    │
│                           Relationships and           │
│                           Perceptions                 │
│                                                       │
└─────────────────────────────────────────────────────┘
```

If you have enjoyed growing up and moving in a world of loving relationships, you will understand why healthy people are surrounded by a network of about twenty people. I describe that "hand-held trampolene" in *Bonding: Relationships in the Image of God*. That relatively small number of significant others remains fairly constant from before birth up into the top productive years of the mid-life decades. The faces change, but the numbers remain the same. By our fifties, however, our networks tend to be shrinking as distance and death take their toll.

To begin looking at the WELLness side of this diagram, sketch in the names of people who were unconditionally committed to your well-being, safety, and survival before you were born. Put them at the birth end on the positive side of the time line. Next, write the names of the early childhood contacts you had with other children your age. It is important during the preschool years that children be allowed to solve their own social problems. Many parents make the mistake of consistently solving their children's problems.

By age ten, special friendships tend to form for healthy girls and boys. Ray, by accepting a parenting role with troubled peers, suffered from a lack of normal experience with peers. Girls are a little more likely than boys to form exclusive friendships. If two girls are "always together," for example, they will begin to share their secrets. Boys are more likely to cluster in small groups of three to five, but they too go for privacy and for sharing secrets. In Ray's case, it was unlikely that as a baby-sitter he would share significant parts of his personal life with the only social contact he had at school. This "homo-social" phase of childhood social development is an important time to lay the foundations for relational skills which will shape later "hetero-social" comfort, dating, and marriage.

Paul Tournier, in his book *Secrets*, describes the need of the very young child to have the gift of "respected privacy." A child needs a private drawer that is not invaded, not even for once a year cleaning. Better yet, a locked box can give a sense of security for the strange and often worthless treasures of the very young. Tournier insists that the child's sense of individuality is closely related to the amount of respected privacy the youngster was given. Around age ten, during transition into adolescence, the child begins to share these secrets. This may involve opening the locked box or digging through the private drawer in the presence of trusted others. This sharing of secrets includes verbal secrets, shared personal experiences, questions, fears, and violations of taboos. To the axiom "best friends know" we can easily add, "best friends never tell." Here, Tournier reminds us, the individual is transformed into a person, because in this Christian psychiatrist's view, people always become persons in·relation to others. Tournier describes how the confidential friendships of teenage years are preparation for the exclusive, lifelong covenant we enter into in a one-flesh, one-mind marriage. For it is only in marriage that we are loved and "known as we are known" in "ultimate naked honesty."[1]

Track yourself on the time line through early childhood, into secrecy, and into the disclosures made to your circle of intimate friends. In completing the chart, you may find it rewarding to identify those special friends who served as midwives on your delivery to a healthy adulthood.

If you are married, note that on the chart and reflect on whether the marriage brought you to the wonderful honesty based on sharing secrets. Then, follow Paul Tournier one more step. Repentance and conversion are the ultimate disclosure according to Tournier. They mark the point in life when we are willing to bring our secret self to God for His blessing and cleansing. If you have a repentance or ultimate truth-telling event, put it on the time line.

Now look at the WARP side of the diagram—the world of abnormal relationships and perceptions. If you suffered from damaging relationships at any point in your lifespan, pinpoint those years when you felt the pain and its aftereffects. Put a secret symbol on the time line representing the actual nature of those abnormal relationships—where violence, abuse, or pain were experienced.

I have used the word "perceptions" to try to capture a subtle reality. My perception of an event or a relationship delivers deep and appropriate feelings to me, in spite of the fact that I may be misreading the intentions of the people relating to me. If I feel discriminated against, put down, or abused, even though these are inappropriate judgments on my part, the effects on me will be much the same as if I was, in fact, violated. One reason many children are spared from great trauma in early childhood is that they naively perceived their parents as loving, generous, and kind, when, in fact, they may have been abusive, domineering, and emotionally damaging.

If the world of the infant is unstable and unpredictable, and if basic needs for security, food, and comfort are not consistently provided, the child will grow learning to cope in extraordinary ways. In extreme cases children can become so confused and frightened by early instability that they fail to thrive and die young. Survivors tend to put up walls against the source of their pain—the people around them. Gary Smalley and John Trent have written powerfully in *The Blessing*, about the positive effects of being blessed by parents as well as the trauma of sensing that you missed their undivided attention.

Introduce physical violence into the young child's world, or punctuate that world with emotional abuse, threats of abandonment, or harassment and there will be crippling effects. Less common, but profoundly devastating, is sexual assault and abuse.

NURTURING MALENESS AND MASCULINITY
Garth, age eight, blurted out the excitement of having a new girlfriend. The family, in the middle of the evening

meal, burst into a mockery of Garth's straightforward but tender information. He never again shared his "best news," and, indeed, drove his attraction for girls underground. He blushed and felt ashamed whenever feelings of love stirred within. I met him twenty years later when he shared his story of inappropriate sexual behavior, one that continued to plague him into young adulthood.

Boys are profoundly more fragile in their sense of sexual identity and sex-appropriate behavior than are girls. In chapter 1 I outlined the sequence of development by which a basically "female" fetus is modified into a male as a boy is brought into the world. Since the standard model of genital and brain formation, including sexual orientation in the brain, is the female model, males are merely a modification of the female version.

Powerful male hormones, androgens, do their part in developing the male. The mother's supply of them accomplished the male genital transformation. And the little male fetus does his part in providing a tiny trickle of androgens, including some of the mighty testosterone, by the twelfth or thirteenth week of development as the testicles begin their performance. By pubescence, the massive charges of male hormones arising out of the boy's sex system provide compelling demands and matching energy to pull the young male toward sex-appropriate behavior.

During the critical early adolescent years it is crucial that a young man's sexual energy be irrevocably connected to his feelings and affections. Yet these are the years when sexual exploitation tries to lure him into the act apart from affection whether by using the *Playboy* centerfold as a masturbation stimulus, by securing sexual service from an adult bookstore, or by stealing sexual pleasure from acquaintances. These are also the years when a young man's sexual energy easily laminates itself to sexually explicit language, four-letter words, and obscenities in general. To the extent that these violent and impersonal stimuli come early and consistently in a young man's life they may create a lifetime attraction to such impersonal and artificial experiences, whether they be on paper, in film, or part of the imagination.

Family affirmation of the young awakening male is crucial. It is important to nurture his capacity for friendship and bolster his confidence in his budding masculinity. If we are intentional about it, we will find appropriate opportunities to give him positive feedback. He needs to know that he is attractive and someday could make a fine husband and father. These sexual roles are the positive alternatives to the popular culture's seduction of his sexual energy by violence, casual sex, and pornography.

Sexual identity is not an automatic gift of biology. By sexual identity I refer to the interior sense of a person's judgments about himself or herself: I am a male. I am a female. These are epochal perceptions that each of us will make about ourselves. We will either make statements affirming ourselves or else question our sexuality in less certain terms: I sometimes wonder whether I am OK as a male? I wonder whether I am acceptable as a female?

Sexual identity is largely formed by the significant people in a boy's life experience. Parents, grandparents, siblings, and friends of the family all play strategic roles. Those people provide feedback on the boy's sex-appropriate behavior.

Gary's father tacked the nickname of "Fairy" onto a beautiful and introverted little boy. It took Gary to age thirty to shake loose from the homosexual innuendo of his father's crude label. His father evidently based the label on the small-boned, fragile looking structure of the little toddler. What seemed like a game to an often drunken father became a damaging and crippling stumbling block for Gary as he voyaged through pubescence with the public shame of the nickname.

When a family friend, trusted perhaps more than any other, and perhaps motivated by the "Fairy" nickname, seduced sixteen-year-old Gary into a single homosexual experience, the label became a tangible albatross around his neck. But as a father of two children, deeply devoted to his wife and with no trace of homosexual preference, it became important for Gary to reconstruct his sexual. identity from the very earliest days. This was accomplished in the protective atmosphere of one of our nurturing groups.

In a sex-crazed and often confused culture, it is clear that certain guidelines must be followed to aid boys in finding their sexual identity. Let me suggest a few:

1. Make it a priority to give young boys significant time and access to the important man in their lives. If Dad is not always available, place the child in close proximity to significant male relatives, or surrogate father options. Churches with a strong sense of community can often provide such options in cases where the father is missing.

2. Affirm every gender-appropriate piece of imitation. Little boys spontaneously walk, talk, and grow up following what Dad does. These are "high-fidelity" moments that need to be enjoyed and nurtured. The child needs to know that his partnership of imitation with Dad is received by the father and celebrated by the mother and significant others.

3. Affirm the quest for acceptance and admiration from a female peer. Actually this is only a special case of further imitation, since wanting to be like Dad is to be joined to a woman. The good news Garth shared at the family dinner table was offered as a way of saying, I want to grow up to be a husband and father. Today I found a girl who might be my wife someday. It was a very serious statement indeed for an eight-year-old boy.

TO BE A FRIEND

Harry Harlow's famous studies with monkeys demonstrated that peer friendship appears to be very important for adolescent primates. He gave names to a half dozen or more specific characteristics of peer love. In his tape series, *Speaking of Love,* Harlow observes, with a bit of sadness, that we have no words to describe a similar human need practiced on the way to maturity. The way in which young girls depend on other girls and boys on other boys for serious and supportive friendship is a critical developmental stage among humans that reflects Harlow's primate discoveries. To be deprived of peer friendship is to be deformed as an adult.

When Manny signed up for a campus appointment where I was a visiting lecturer, I was startled at his youthfulness.

"How old are you?" I began.

"Sixteen."

"How do you get to be a college freshman at sixteen?"

"My parents were missionaries, so I did a lot of my work in home schooling. I want to talk about the loneliness I feel around here. Someday I'm sure I'll be ready for bonding, and all of those things you write and talk about, but right now I need a guy friend."

I listened carefully to this primal cry for friendship. Yes, he said, there was one guy in orchestra that he really wanted to be close to. But then he confided, "He's dating, and I can't ask him to spend time with me. It wouldn't be right to cut in on them."

I couldn't get his age off my mind, so I pressed him for a time line. Where had he lived and was he in home schooling between ages nine and fourteen? You guessed it. He was essentially locked away from peer contact, and starved for significant friendship at a time when male development suffers profoundly if held in a vacuum. We wound up our appointment time with a game plan to bring three guys, not one, into a fellowship group that would include weekend activities together. It is not uncommon for young men with empty spots in their peer network during early adolescence to suffer deeply from feelings of social isolation and frustration.

Del asked for personal conference time at a national

youth conference. I thought he was one of the college-age counselors. At about six foot four and apparently very at ease with the counseling staff, I was not prepared for the truth. When Del showed up I discovered he had recently turned seventeen, and was going into his senior year of high school the next month. "That's unbelievable!" I said, astounded. "You could get away with telling me you were twenty-one!"

I had not known Del long when he asked a question I am never quite prepared for, "How do I learn to love? I don't think I am a loving person. A lot of people offer friendship to me, but I keep them away."

Although I rarely anticipate this inner condition of loneliness, especially in beautiful people, my response was ready from long and effective use: "How do you like being who you are?"

"I try not to think about that."

"Whatever for?" I probed.

"Because it would be indulging in pride—it would seem selfish."

"What if I told you that your problem with reaching out to others is that you have refused to like yourself? That's hard for me to imagine, at one level, because you are so poised and at peace. You dress intentionally and tastefully, and you present yourself so positively in public. But on another level I hear what you are saying. We have done a good job of knocking the pride out of any willing disciple and demanding passive humiliation in our church tradition. So you have taken us seriously—perhaps too seriously."

I suggested to Del that Jesus formulated the rule: those who do not love themselves will be unable to love other people. "Love your neighbor as yourself" (Matt. 22:39) appears to be a command, but it is more likely an axiom or a general principle. It may even be a warning that you will be unable to love other people until you have a deep respect and thankfulness for being yourself. In a way much like we find in the Matthew 7:1 axiom, loving may cut both ways. Remember? "Do not judge, or you too will be judged."

"Come with me," I said to Del. I took him to a large mirror. "Look at those guys," I said as the two of us stood side by side. "What do you see?"

"A tall skinny kid with acne. He has skinny arms—no biceps at all."

"What else?"

"He slouches too much—needs to stand up straighter."

"Can I tell you what I see?"

He was bracing himself against my probable praise. I did not carry much weight with Del. He had met me only three days before, and then only as 1 of 2,000 people in a massive teaching session. Real clout comes from people with long-term contact. It is parents who make the greatest mark on the emerging sense of self-respect.

"I see a guy I thought was a college man, and one of the counselors here. Now that I've met him personally, I still find myself surprised that he could show so much dignity and quality at such an early age. But then, the same mistakes were made with me when I was seventeen. I think it came from some of the suffering I went through in high school. Your older brother has been a worry to you, I know. Maybe that has ripened you too."

My affirmation caught him off guard. It wasn't the glib praise he had expected, and I could tell I had caught his attention at a very deep level.

"Give yourself permission to look in the mirror every morning and pray out loud with your eyes open. Thank God that He has created you Del King. Form a prayer of thanksgiving something like this, 'I don't know why You did it or what You have in mind for me, but I thank You that You made me just like I am. I am grateful for the body You gave me, out of all of the millions of genetic possibilities I might have become. I am thankful to be a male. I celebrate the good mind You gave me, and for getting my attention when I was young, so You could start early making me into the person You created me to become."

THE TIGER ROARS
Del showed a remarkable ability to cope, at seventeen, with a fully adult body. At six-foot four, looking like he was in his twenties, with traces of acne still on both cheeks, he was the picture of the ideal emerging adult male. For reasons that are not entirely clear, the male hormone which saturates the baby boy from the ninth week of his conception, continues to dictate profound realities in his body. These realities are witnessed in a number of significant areas of the male makeup.

Active energy. From first fetal movement to mid-life, the male hormonal charge kicks males into higher activity levels than females. In *Bonding: Relationships in the Image of God*, I have described how energetic young boys are often penalized, especially in school and church classes. Young boys need action; to put them in crowded environments which demand long periods of passive silence violates everything that makes up a boy. In the early elementary years, it is common for teachers to request that parents get medication for their hyperactive sons, when in most cases their activity needs are well within the normal range. The number of children that should be handled by an adult boils down to this formula, never more critical than in handling young boys: one adult per the average age of the children. For example, eight children with an average age of four would require two adults to care for them. In a church nursery class, the department should be staffed by assigning one adult for every three or four children.

Bone structure. Unlike giant redwoods, humans grow to maturity and stop. While human growth is still shrouded in partial mystery, we do know that each bone in the human body carries a stop signal near the end of the bone section which signals maximum length permitted. We worry when a child breaks a leg, for example, lest the signal system be thrown off and uneven growth occur.

Males develop into slightly larger—that is, taller and thicker—skeletal models than corresponding females. Let me say it another way. Should the conception have carried exactly the same genetic material except for the gender selecting X or Y chromosome combinations, the XX version would have been slightly smaller in stature and in bone formation than the XY male version. While part of the difference is in the genetic gender specifications, most of it is likely the result of the mother's male hormones pumped into fetal development and the long-term effects of the boy's own androgens. The volatile testosterone associated with the higher activity and restlessness levels in boys is especially at work.

Single-mindedness. I described the androgen bath boys' brains get in the sixteenth to twenty-sixth week of fetal development in chapter 1. Looking at male behavior, it is no surprise to discover that the damage to the corpus colossum and to the left hemisphere becomes visible. For one thing, the typical right-handed, right-eye-dominant male deals with almost everything in a rational way. He rarely talks about his feelings, emotions, beliefs, or aesthetic judgments. Those parts of life are locked away in the undamaged but hungry right hemisphere, and they are not often put into words—which must be formulated in the left hemisphere. Another result, given the ability to block out their personal sides, is that males tend to become experts at keeping their minds on their business. They can easily focus on things they choose while ignoring their environment. In contrast to the typical female who processes everything through both affective and cognitive hemispheres (right and left), men are more likely to hunker down through their analytical left hemisphere operations.

In one sense, these left-brain-dominant operations seem to show the male as damaged and partial in his abilities. But we need to look through this crack in his

83

To Be Himself

armor to see that he does, indeed, have feelings, care about beliefs and values, and is able to respond to claims in those domains. When the typical man feels deeply and shuts down his efficient problem-solving logic, he may be reduced to tears and seem to have lost control. You will see his feelings, often shamelessly presented to you. But when his capacity to love, to embrace truth, make an irreversible commitment to God, or to feel the peak experience in a dramatic or musical presentation, is summoned, he is likely to be speechless. Even later, he may be unable to verbalize what he was feeling, even though he was visibly in the grip of a profound yet unexplainable inner reality.

Knowing this great capacity of a man for giving himself to the grandest human vision, Jesus packaged His message in significant stories and parables. Men have little resistance to a story or to a generous and grand enactment of truth. So Jesus surrounded Himself with men of deep and profound commitment, and still does. As men follow stories, their right hemisphere is activated and their values are carried along into revision. But when the Pharisees, exclusively men, would arrive to try to trick Jesus, they used left-brained single-minded logical strategies, thus deliberately shutting down their beliefs and values, to keep themselves safely out of touch from Jesus' convicting teaching.

I referred to men's hungry right hemisphere with its feelings, images, creativity, and convictions. Their need for right brain stimulation no doubt accounts for the ways they listen to music, their fascination with stories which picture humorous events, and their vulnerability to those who pose moral or spiritual dilemmas in story or parable form. We will understand men better if we see their "single-mindedness" and their "speechless" responses as unique revelations of what men really are. And if any movement or congregation falters in its appeal to attract males to its ranks, you can bet that they do not understand the uniqueness of the human male.

Sexual pleasure. If you could see the Ciba medical drawing of genital development, you would note that the pleasure center of the baby girl, the clitoris, reduces in relative size from the ninth week of fetal development until birth. At nine weeks, the pleasure center in the male and female are identical, are raised external to the body, and relatively large. They are magnified again and both appear to be developing into an external penis in the twelfth week. Then the clitoris shrinks and is enfolded within the vaginal lips by birth and the head of the penile shaft is greatly enlarged. Not only is the size of the pleasure center profoundly larger in the boy, it will magnify again at the onset of pubescence. This sensitive sexual pleasure organ is mounted on the end of the penile shaft which houses the urinary tract. This means that a male must deal explicitly with this high pleasure part of his anatomy at each urination event.

Cross-cultural examinations of the way males deal with the penis indicate the central place it plays in coming to manhood. The ancient Jews brought the penis under God's control through a rite of circumcision. This tangible, physical reminder of God's covenant would be a very personal reminder to every Jewish boy of his special sexual accountability to God. The circumcised Jewish penis, should it turn up in inappropriate places such as a house of prostitution, would witness against the male and accuse him of infidelity.

Among the Dani tribe in New Guinea, a phallic stick made of a hollow gourd is placed over the penis at the male rite of passage. This sudden change of status is initiated when the external male genitalia become obviously mature. In this naked tribe the marks of maturity are easily visible with the budding breasts of the girls and the enlarging phallus and testicles of the male. The phallic stick may extend to several inches above the head of the male if he is of royal blood, or may be a modest waist height in a common born male.

The phallic stick is the only "garment" the male will

To Be Himself

ever wear, except when he adds war regalia to his head and war paint to his body. The phallic stick is held in place by a tree root string which loops down the long gourd which houses the penis and wraps around the base of the scrotum. This drawstring effect is then tied at the top end of the gourd; more tree-root cord is used to tie the upright penis stick around the waist for the shorter models and around the armpits for the regal versions. As an indicator of status the phallic stick displays a mighty extension to the penis, but as a public accountability symbol, it denotes that this penis is under tribal surveillance. The death penalty applies to any young male who breaks protocol by prematurely using his penis with a woman. No questions are asked. The question does not revolve around whether a pregnancy may have occurred. Cultures which institute a death penalty for premature or inappropriate sexual contact are addressing the "out of control" possibilities. They recognize that the pleasure center can dominate the life of a male, unless it is brought under community control and personal accountability for responsible use.

I met Doug at a family camp when he was fifteen. He reported to me, when I saw him during his college freshman year, that during his first twenty-four hours on campus, he was solicited by the college gay organization. During that same day he was also propositioned by an attractive, obviously seasoned senior woman, "How would you like to come to my apartment tonight and use your body?"

Doug's initiation invitations are an increasingly common temptation to young males. It is clear that a culture which exploits this pleasure potential in its young males and which urges them to use their penises for their own private satisfaction, is sending its young men in the pursuit of addictive destruction. Such a society is just as certainly committing cultural suicide.

Fertility. The gift of "life," through the arrival of sexual ripening at pubescence, is easily the most treasured feature of sexual identity—for both healthy boys and girls. When they contemplate the possibility that they could "make a baby," they are looking at the power of their own creative fertility.

We are part of a culture which has trivialized the fertility of the young. We see more attention to fertility as the enemy than as the gift of life, that mystery of creative energy which enhances the value of being human. Our fear of the fertility of the young has us focused on birth control devices and abortion. But among the young, there is a wonder and celebration which often has to be carried on secretly as if it were illegal and forbidden contraband.

The arrival of menstruation is a marker for the young woman, and is commonly an event known among close family members. But the male's arrival at first ejaculation is often only inferred by parents or peers based on his sudden elevation in height or the appearance of facial and body hair.

Recalling the genital development discussion from chapter 1, you will remember the ovary/testicle part of the original anatomy. In the female these sources of fertility remain on location and shift into a horizontal position. At maturity the ovary will begin to release ripened seeds or ovum. Each ovary will ripen one seed about every fifty-six days, and the ovaries will alternate their ripening cycle so that in half that time—about twenty-eight days—first one, then the other, will release an egg.

When the ovary was transformed into a testicle and the pair were dropped into the vaginal-lip scrotum with the magical seal enclosing them and providing the sheath for the penis, the nature of the ovary was changed. Instead of releasing the "seed of the original woman," which is the gift of life transmitted through the ovum, the testicle development actually activates a factory for producing sperm—the male seed. While the woman's ovaries are prepackaged with a limited number of ovum—more than she could possibly use in the thirty-five to forty years of her fertility, sperm production in the male is virtually unlimited. There is no age limit, no menopause to shutdown male fertility. The sperm are produced "from scratch," carrying no tracer back to "the original mother" as the ovum does. Beyond all of this, sperm are produced in absolutely incredible quantities. Consider the following minimums.

1. A healthy male will release about 300 million live sperm with every ejaculation. Extravagance is written everywhere in this aspect of human fertility, because only one of those sperm could normally survive through meeting the ovum and joining to form a baby. The other hundreds of millions were just spares to guarantee delivery of at least one tremendous "strong wiggler" who beat all of the others to the available egg waiting around in the fallopian tube.

2. The typical male is ripening that sperm harvest on an average of every forty-eight hours.

3. First ejaculation, at an average age of thirteen years and three months, is typically followed by thirty-six months of increasing frequency of ejaculation which tends to set the adult appetite for pleasure and to reveal the healthy adult capacity for male fertility production. Sperm and seminal fluids, all laced with various levels of the androgens, especially testosterone, are the lively activity fuel which drive males when their restlessness is compared to females. The sperm count, the amount of ejaculate produced, and the frequency of ejaculation vary widely among mature males.[2]

This "tiger in the tank" is likely the least understood but most treasured gift of God to the healthy male. When I explained all of this nearly twenty years ago in a parent seminar at Hamburg Wesleyan Church in New York, I rounded out the biological material with a universal anecdote: "When Johnny reaches sexual maturity, it is Mother who most often finds traces of his masturbation or wet dreams, and Mother knows what ejaculate is when she sees it. So Mother says to Dad, 'You've got to talk to Johnny.' And Dad says he'll do it. But he doesn't. Do you know why Dad doesn't say anything to his son?" I asked.

I continued, "It is because Dads are basically honest people, and they haven't yet figured out their own sexuality. So they stall. They simply can't bring themselves to lie to their sons. Silence is better than pretending that they have the answers, when they still have serious questions themselves."

Suddenly I heard the clatter of two chairs to my right. I stopped and stared into the faces of two men who had stiffened in their folding chairs, feet banging chairs accordion-style, in front of them. They had the look of men who had been ambushed by the police, caught red-handed in their crime. "Is there something wrong?" I questioned.

"I can't believe you know the scenario. We've just been through this at our house," one of the men volunteered. I wasn't surprised.

I conclude that the gift of fertility is God's first curriculum. It calls the young man to accept full responsibility for regulating his pleasure, treasuring his fertility for personal, community, and eternal purposes, to harness his entire sexual energy in service of a lifelong, exclusive relationship with one woman whereby the two will become one. It is not good for any human to be alone is the primal wail of every healthy male.

TO BE IN LOVE

In the best of all possible worlds a young man sees, meets, and falls in love with a woman. Then he finds that she was orchestrating the whole thing all along because she had her own reasons for stalking him. Sexual energy and the search for love provokes males to a more complete use of the full brain than any other pursuit. In any social or cultural system a healthy man's dream of sexual pleasure unites with the high energy to be independent and responsible as an adult male. To these visions is added the distinct desire to be a father, that is, to extend his identity into time and eternity through the responsible management of his gift of fertility. Because of this great "desire" he takes initiatives, sometimes surprisingly assertive where he has been introverted in other contexts, and the "pair" appears. This consummation leads to the matching of life vision with an exclusive life with one woman. With vocation and marriage in tact, the circle is complete.

Most men have major chunks of unfinished business in hidden sexual secrets. Many of us have had neither a vocabulary to describe our sexual behavior, nor any sense of the source of the sexual energy. Human sexuality is shrouded in a veil of important privacy, but in that protected place it has often suffered in silence. I have sought to furnish a biological picture of developing male sexuality to connect the sex system to intrinsic male needs and motivations. And by comparing male and female development, I have wanted to offer a way for any man to face the woman of his dreams and sense that this baffling "otherness" is profoundly "bone of bone, flesh of flesh," the same stuff though radically different.

George Gilder may be right. Males may be only occasionally "sexual" compared to the holistic female connection to her sexuality, though I think he defines male sexuality too superficially. But if males are only occasionally aware of their yearning for sexual intimacy, their sexual energy drives them day and night for a lifetime, and the years from ten to one hundred tend to be very sexually oriented in their priority for males. So, while there are many "unfinished business" agendas for men, the first and central arena where men often remain crippled is in their failure to come to honest terms with their sexual appetite, its energy, and their need for intimacy based on absolute mutual respect. The chapters which follow will never stray far from this sexual core of male identity and need.

FIVE

◊

BONDING
FOR LIFE

Every spring at Asbury Seminary I teach a course called "Discipleship Development in the Home." Each season, a part of the curriculum of reading and reflecting examines things that have gone wrong with families. Last spring, a team of three presenters were all single young adults. One surprised even herself by making a disclosure of childhood sexual abuse. Another had been profoundly damaged by a broken engagement. A third, coming from a single-parent urban home, had been traumatized in ways at which he only hinted. All expressed serious reservations whether marriage and family life, inviting as they were in the abstract, could likely deliver the goods for a satisfying long-term prospect.

I sensed a cloud of empathetic grief and sadness hovering over the room of nearly fifty students, so in the closing moments, I said, "Is there a married person here who would like to say a word of hope to these folks?" I have a high tolerance for ambiguity, and the bleakness of prospect we had experienced for more than forty minutes was a perspective worth contemplating. Still, I am an eternal optimist so I cast my line upon the sea of faces. There were no volunteers, but I saw Chris Kiesling about ten feet from me with a grin and a glow that made my invitation a safe bet, so I gambled.

"What good word can you give them, Chris? You and Suzanne have been married now for more than a year."

In an instant, his response began, and even though class was ready to end, his words were terse and piercing: "Everything about our marriage and wedding was a revisitation of my conversion."

The roomful of students was entranced by that single sentence, spoken softly in response to a professor's probe. Chris went on, "In marriage there is a completion of yourself. There is a making of a commitment to live completely under the scrutiny of another person. It is as if 'iron sharpens iron,' as Proverbs 27:17 says, yet the alteration of identity and self comes in the midst of a gentle, warm relationship. What you can find in marriage that you can't find in being single is a relationship where you can risk being completely honest. You can be fully exposed and vulnerable and still find the intimacy of knowing you are in the arms of a person who loves and cares for you unconditionally."

The bell rang. Everyone was stunned. The panel of discouraged presenters remained seated at the front of the room behind me. Chris' peers filed out in silence. I finally recovered enough to say something affirming. Then I asked, "Where did that come from?"

"Well, as usual, there is a story behind it."

"Can we hear it tomorrow?"

"Sure."

"Remind me at the beginning of class, and we'll look into your heart at what about your marriage reminded you of your conversion."

I went ahead with the class agenda the next day. Chris, characteristic of him, did not remind me to let him finish his story. But near the end of the period, I caught a glimpse of Chris and remembered. So I introduced him, inviting him to the front of the room.

"Yesterday, Chris blew us all away by revisiting his marriage to Suzanne and disclosing that its culmination was a revisitation of his conversion. I learned that there is a story behind the theology he opened up for us. I have no idea what it is, but here's Chris."

Chris began slowly, "One day when Suzanne and I were dating, she was baby-sitting for Steve and Thanne Moore's baby boy, Madison. The Moores were the directors of the Wesley Foundation where we had met. She had been with Madison all day, and I went up late that day, eager to see Suzanne, but also wanting some time with Madison. I had not done much baby-sitting, so I looked forward to practicing my fathering skills. Suzanne had been having a lot of fun all afternoon with him. She wanted me to have a little experience with the baby. Suzanne handed Madison to me. Immediately he began to cry. I could not find a way to quiet him. Suzanne eventually took him back to his room and put him in his crib.

"In the brief time that elapsed a kind of rush came over me. I realized that I had the potential of being a good father, but had never been put in a situation where I could try it. To be in a situation where I had that opportunity, and for the child to burst out with what seemed like a total rejection of me, released an avalanche of lifelong episodes of rejection. I felt like Madison's rejection of me was not based on anything I had done to him, but was simply his rejection of me as a person—because of who I was.

"I collapsed on the couch, and I began thinking of the experiences of humiliation I had been through. I remembered a time in junior high school when I was asked to crown the cheerleader elected as Valentine's Day queen. It was expected that I would give her a big kiss with everyone applauding after I had placed the crown on her head. But, losing my nerve, I simply pecked her on the cheek. The beginning crescendo of applause for the queen turned into a violent *boo* from my fellow classmates. I walked back to the bleachers surrounded by this wall of *boos*. I remembered how humiliating that was.

"I remembered too feeling like I was a hopeless weakling in ninth grade. I was a tall kid, and the coaches yelled at me, humiliating and degrading me because I was not able to lift weights well enough to satisfy them. All of this humiliation of my past began washing over me like a tidal wave. Overwhelmed, I lay there on the couch in the director's living room crying. Immobilized, I collapsed and shook with sobbing, remembering the many rejections I had experienced.

"Suzanne came in from the other room, sat down, and put my head in her lap and just let me cry. She simply held me. I relaxed completely. Slowly I realized that there was no reason in the world why I deserved that childhood rejection. I saw that everything ugly and vile that I had suffered was suddenly exposed to Suzanne. Yet she was saying, 'It's OK. I love you.' To me it was the most profound experience of pure grace I had ever experienced from another person. I began to understand what it is not to earn, not to feel like there was some performance I had to demonstrate, before I was worthy of love. Here was a complete relinquishment of everything I was to another person—in my ugliest moments of painful memory—accompanied by Suzanne's acceptance expressed simply and freely, 'It's OK. I love you'!"

Then Chris, turning to some of the students who had expressed serious questions about marriage and fears about leaving singleness, went on saying, "This is not the end of my story. Before I was reduced to emotional nakedness in front of Suzanne, there was only one other place that I was experiencing grace. That was in my times alone with the Lord. This led me to wrestle with the apparent contradiction between my need for companionship with Suzanne and my need for solitude and private devotion to God.

"I was then reading Mike Mason's classic *The Mystery of Marriage*. He tells the story of his struggle between becoming a monk and getting married. The book opens as he is taking his new bride to visit the Trappist monastery where he had been accepted to become a monk. Mike Mason had worked with the contradiction in a way I was not having to do. In his tradition, he struggled between mutually exclusive choices—between the call to solitude and grace or the call of love and marriage. But he saw that the call to become a celibate monk and the call to marriage are essentially the same call. In both cases Mike would have to surrender everything. Both monastic orders and marriage are calls to give the self away.

"So, I saw that there was really no contradiction for me either. If I pitted my privacy and total devotion to God as a single male against love and marriage, I had not understood the integrity required of me to be totally devoted to God and single. To remain single as an act of freedom to fit my own scheme, even for devotion to God, would ultimately be an act of arrogance and privatism. I saw that whether I chose singleness to perfectly practice my devotion to God or marriage, I would end up in the same place. I discovered that I would really find myself only when I gave myself away, with no strings attached. The difference might be that the single person could find that surrender through solitude and through enduring a private Gethsemane. But the married person might expect to find it through shared companionship and walking through the marriage vows in a kind of corporate Gethsemane.

"What grace did for me through Suzanne after flunking the fathering test, reminded me of the painful realities behind the Superman stories. A mediocre news reporter who often missed the big story and muffed details in embarrassing ways, who was weak, incompetent and never destined to achieve greatness, also had a great secret. No one knew how he did it, but he could, in the face of a major catastrophe, slip into a telephone booth, change clothes, and emerge with a red cape and super-human powers.

"In my experience, somewhere down the line, I suspect that I will find freedom from my own feelings of weakness, incompetence, and inhibition. Chris Kiesling may actually perform incredible acts of servanthood and ministry. In my imagination I see my spirit taking off, soaring and 'leaping over tall buildings in a single bound.' And, in my dreams, I think that I will be able to look back and identify the 'phone booth' where I was reduced to nakedness, shedding the ordinary clothes that represent my weakness. My feelings of inferiority and humiliation evaporated there, and I was able to slip into special super clothes. I'm sure that when I turn to look at the 'phone booth,' its illuminated sign will read simply, Marriage."

IDEAL BONDING

Chris gave us a picture-window view into one of the final closure events in his pursuit of marriage with Suzanne. His experience is enough to suggest some main lines in a theology of marriage. Chris was healed from damaging memories and devastation; this caused him to gain a new self-esteem. But we know that their relationship began long before that moment of vulnerability through humiliation. They must have spent their entire lives getting ready to be unconditionally "present" to each other.

Imagination. The vision of life fulfilled through an exclusive, lifelong intimacy is buried deep in the heart of every growing child. From infancy, given access to both a father and a mother, children infer the hope that somewhere, sometime there will be an "opposite" to love them, to hold them, to make life tolerable, and to share its ecstasies. I use the word "imagination" to describe future possibilities based on present realities. Chris and Suzanne must have had a "curriculum" of trust surrounding them from childhood. From the building blocks of early relationships they could "image" a future in which intimacy sealed a new unit. It could never fully prepare them for the vulnerability, or the unconditional accepting and acceptance that might be involved, but they were ready.

Relationship. In the ideal scenario, a young couple will each be in touch with their real sense of "need." There is a cosmic loneliness that hangs like a cloud of hope motivating the search for the "other." There is the time invested before a mirror asking the urgent question, *Will there be anyone who will love me for who I am? I can never make myself into a desirable person unless someone sees more in me than I see in myself.*

During our own long months of engagement, separated from Robbie by a thousand miles, I tuned my radio at 11 o'clock each night, eager to hear the theme music and poetry featured on the radio show, "Moon River," which I could sometimes pick up from Cincinnati. I bought the 78 rpm record of Mary Carolyn Davies' litany of love, which I heard often on "Moon River." In answer to her question, "Why do I love you?" I could resonate with the incredibly plausible response, "I love you not only for what you are, but for what I am when I am with you." The reality of my own emotional bankruptcy engulfed me each time the lines reached the crescendo: "I love you because you are helping me to build of the lumber of my life not a tavern but a temple."

The sense of vulnerability and dependency are all but overwhelming in the solitude of the human condition. C.S. Lewis, in an amazing but little-noticed poem entitled "As the Ruin Falls," suggests that it is the awakening of profound love for another that reveals the past self-centeredness of all of life. It was all simply "flashy rhetoric about loving you," he confesses. "I never had a selfless thought since I was born." Trapped inside his own skin, it is love that has drawn him out, until his heart is being fashioned into a "bridge" to reach his beloved and thus to embrace mature manhood. And now, even though the bridge is breaking, he says, "The pains you give me are more precious than all other gains." 'Indeed, to become human and to have the dignity of loving and being loved is worth whatever risks of pain that might come. Healthy loving always focuses on the person, not on any of the rewards that might be stolen from another simply to satisfy an appetite.

Conversation. The original male was provoked to the first coherent human speech by the sight of the newly formed woman: "This is now bone of my bones and flesh of my flesh; she shall be called Ishah, for she was taken out of Ish" (Gen. 2:23, my translation). In a similar way, every male is called out of his silence by the attraction of a special woman. Young men, who rarely speak a complete sentence to their parents, can talk by the hour to magnetic women who call them to rise above their brains' damaged speech center and to join their feelings to their words. Some males write poetry only during their high romance period of life. Occasionally they will be inspired to set words to music. Strange and wonderful emotions arise, providing the energy that characterizes the dialogue of young men in love.

Touch. We nuzzle our babies, cuddle our toddlers, and wrestle with our young children. But when boys hit pubescence in this culture, they typically pull back, distancing themselves from parents and adults who would still like to hug them. We get to touch our teenage sons and grandsons in ritual moments, those hellos and good-byes provide virtually the only moments during which a quick hug can occur. It is as if they are intentionally on a "fast," abstaining from the much-needed physical expression because of an intuition that sometime, somewhere, someone will come along who can satisfy the gnawing "skin hunger" that keeps them vulnerable as they launch into the search for love.

Intimacy. If marriage can be characterized by "knowing as we are known," then Chris and Suzanne were on

Unfinished Business

the threshold of marriage, but could hardly have known it when Chris collapsed into his deep memories of humiliation. Suzanne was seeing Chris as he really was. He may be her Superman, but he will never be fantastic in the sense of being unreal. His strength will rise from the reality of his vulnerability and his revisitation of his memories of rejection and helplessness.

Paul Pearsall, in his *Super Marital Sex: Loving for Life*, reminds us that super marriages are based on absolute transparency and disclosure. The intimacy we all need must be built from a foundation of honesty, not by masquerading our weaknesses or past adventures. Pearsall, having studied one thousand couples with five-year follow-up in his Problems of Daily Living Clinic at Detroit's Sinai Hospital, concludes that intimacy must be built on complete honesty between the marital couple. Pearsall also currently serves as the director of professional education for the Kinsey Institute for Research in Sex, Gender, and Reproduction. He takes the position that our unmarried young people should not be having sexual intercourse, and that they are damaging their future marriages. "Sex is not like tennis," he notes. "Practice does not make perfect in sex, it only leads to more practice."[2] It turns out that "more practice" in sex is practice in promiscuity or divorce, or both.

Pair bonding studies show that genital contact must be postponed until a couple has completed the curriculum of history giving, hammered out their values, and taken full responsibility for the lifelong needs and integrity of their partner. If genital contact precedes these agendas in the twelve-step sequence, the bond will be profoundly weakened and is susceptible to marital failure. Pearsall is giving up-to-date professional and clinical evidence in support of the pair bonding sequence implications.[3]

PREMATURE BONDING
It was a week of luxury; I had lots of free time at a week-long family camp where the schedule provided leader-

ship other than my own. Early in the week, working through the lunch line, I was startled by a young man I had not noticed before. As he turned facing me, virtually shoulder-to-shoulder, I saw his good face and at about fourteen his stunning new manhood was written all over him. Without any introduction at all, I simply blurted out, "I don't know whether anybody has ever told you or not, but you are dangerously good-looking. And if you don't give it all to Jesus, you're in big trouble!"

Evidently, Brad already knew me, the camp grandfather and teacher of an adult seminar. At any rate, my comment triggered a sudden outpouring, "There's this girl who's been chasing me for two days and says she wants to date me," he whispered eagerly.

"See what I mean?" I laughed, and dismissed the exchange.

A day later Brad's mother approached me. I had seen her in all of my sessions, but had not seen her with Brad. "My mother was with Brad when you spoke to him in line yesterday," she reported casually.

I smiled, "That's wonderful. He's an amazingly good-looking young man."

"Well, you really made his day, and ours too," Brad's mother went on. "I really wish my husband could have been here this week, but he couldn't get off work. So I'm here with the children and my mother is along to help. Brad is our oldest. In fact, my mother has never forgiven my husband because I got pregnant with Brad on our high school senior trip. We were both out of good church families, and it crushed them all. We got married, and you now know the rest of the story about the fourteen-year-old boy that came from that misadventure."

The scenario of premature bonding often carries layers of pain, and in this case a very persistent layer of shame. But the chief pain of premature genital contact in a healthy bonding relationship is the "crisis" it brings as two people scramble to guarantee they will never have

Unfinished Business

to say good-bye. They are ready to climb every mountain to protect the forever bond and take it into public display.

"Take along a copy of my *Bonding: Relationships in the Image of God* and read it with your husband," I encouraged her. "You will see your story there—the Bill and Betty story—but your story has a delightfully happier ending than theirs. Congratulations on a super marriage and on a super son. I suspect all of the children are as wholesome as Brad."

Brad's parents were exclusively bonded. They survived pressures from disappointed parents, but the bond only was forged under hotter fire. His parents took full responsibility for their intimacy, and foreclosed their childhood and adolescence in favor of protecting the pregnancy and their own relationship. We rarely see stronger bonds than this, even though they didn't "make it to the church on time." If such couples could be studied systematically, we would surely see this "marriage" of pleasure and responsibility forming an indestructibly tough bond. Couples who abort pregnancies, or who are clever enough to avoid the pregnancy while stealing the pleasure, often live to yearn for integrity like that which welded Brad's parents into a super marriage.

DEALING WITH GHOSTS

I met Carl while lecturing at a university. He first left a message at my hotel. As I read and reread the note I examined Carl's name. Sure enough, his father and I serve on a national board of directors together. His dad had told me of giving my *Bonding* book to a son who was getting married. Carl inquired whether I could save my Wednesday lunch hour to eat with him and his wife.

Carl and Gayle took me to lunch in the college grill. There he reported Gayle's continuing descent into hell as she replayed fantasy scenarios of Carl's late teen escapade of "living in" with an older woman. Carl summarized the painful story of rebellion against his parents, sexual adventure, and trouble and agony. At the end of that rope he came in repentance to Jesus, and eventually in love to Gayle. Before he proposed marriage to Gayle, Carl sought to clear the slate, so he gave her a detailed confession of his three lost years between leaving home and being reconciled to his parents and to his faith. Instead of letting go of the honest disclosure Carl had given her, Gayle seemed to be reviving it and breathing life into it more powerfully every day.

Carl sat there in the campus restaurant, in full view of his peers, his eyes flooding with uncontrolled tears. I watched as he mopped them up with napkins from the table dispenser. "You are married to a remarkable man," I told Gayle. "Diogenes can throw away his lantern. You have found an honest man. Most men would settle for a mediocre marriage rather than going to the root and hauling out the truth of their adolescent rebellion and sexual misadventures. But let me make a prediction," I said to Gayle. "You may be keeping Carl's old adultery alive when he has let it go. In fact, you may be making it more vivid than it ever was to him. And if you can't let it go, it is likely to boomerang on you. You are very likely to develop such resentment that you will plot to get even with Carl. You are going to be vulnerable to having an affair just to hurt Carl. But he has suffered so much for so long that he's less vulnerable to an affair than you will be.

"Let me offer you a strategy. Remember that whatever you are feeling is okay. But it is not okay to revive the ghost of Carl's past adultery, a previous bond now long since buried and dead. I'm going to ask you to write your feelings—toward Carl, toward that three-year-live-in woman, and toward anyone else. You can name them and write as if you were telling them exactly what they have done to you and to your marriage. Send all of them to me and mark the outside of the envelope 'for your files only,' and I will never open it, but you will know that you said it all, once, on paper."

Gayle agreed to write out all of her grievances and to mail the document to me. Three months later, with nothing from Gayle, I wrote to the two of them.

Gayle wrote back immediately: "I'm sorry I did not begin the writing I agreed to do. Thank you for taking me seriously. Two other counselors had told me to forget it, but you said my feelings were important and should be dealt with. But after we talked in the grill that day, it seemed like all of my hurt was gone. If it ever comes back I will write it out and send it to you. Our marriage is healed, I'm sure."

Because sexuality is at the center of our personalities, it is also the first curriculum of our moral responsibility. Everything about sexual feelings and behavior is colored with the ecstasy of the "ultimate good" or the tragic pain of the "ultimate evil." With sexual matters there is very little that falls within the middle ground between good and evil.

This mysterious gift at the core of human existence is the source, all at once, of: (1) personal identity; (2) pleasure; (3) reproduction; (4) the "two into one" glue of pair bonding.

It is this "epoxy bond" by which two people are laminated into one heart, one energy, and one vision.

DEALING WITH CASUAL SEX

"I'm a little uneasy about opening this subject up for you guys who are single, but I need help. It may even be that my experience will mean something to all of you." Dan was taking the floor, at his request, in a support and formation meeting where the unwritten rule is that the first agenda goes to a member in need of solving an immediate problem.

"You know I was married about six months ago, but you don't know that I was sexually active with five other women during my university days. Further, my wife and I had intercourse for about six months before we were married. Sometimes I think of those women when I'm having intercourse with my wife. I feel guilty about that. I know it is not right. But what is really bothering me now is that the buzz just isn't there when we have sex now. It always was before I was married and I hate to think that it's gone forever."

Dan took questions from his peers. Two students discussed parallel accounts of coping with similar postmarital adjustment. "Have you worked on what Dr. Joy calls retroactive healing?" one of the group asked.

"No. What do you mean?" queried Dan.

In response, I unpacked my discovery that the experience of God's sanctification means, among other things, bringing honesty and integrity to all of life here and now. I am no longer put off by that text in 1 Thessalonians 4:3: "For this is the will of God, even your sanctification, that ye should abstain from fornication" (KJV). It is pretty clear both from St. Paul and from human experience that sexual energy is either going to be thrown around in fornication or celebrated in sanctification.

Overcoming life's sexual baggage requires revisiting the painful past and asking God to transform prior experiences. It means letting the God of Creation and Lord of sexual differentiation and pleasure make it whole and holy in your memory.

"Here is what it might mean for you, Dan," I began. "How old were you when you first had genital contact?"

"Seventeen."

"Okay. You are now ready to love Carla exclusively and passionately for the rest of your life. In your own imagination, do this: Whenever one of those old images appears, take Carla back to that event when you were seventeen. Cut away that old image of a woman who must surely be joined to some other man by now anyway. Now 'laser beam' in Carla's image—your lifelong exclusive lover. I call this 'laser beam sanctification surgery of memory.' Imagine that you have only been sexual with Carla. If you do this persistently, it will have a wonderful effect. It will restore your monogamous vision, and it will laminate all of your affection to Carla.

"In addition, do this wild and marvelous thing; imagine that, miracle of miracles, you were married to Carla before you had the contact at seventeen. The cultural rules are suspended, and from your first sexual imagination there has always been Carla—the other side of yourself. The surgery works all the way back to childhood, because imagination transcends legal marriage age and goes for what is true, right, holy, and pure."

Dan and Carla indulged in the luxury of eating the frosting off the cake. They took the pleasure and rejected the responsibility for truly endowing each other with all their earthly goods before consumating the physical intimacy. Their courtship was rocky, and the engagement broke under Dan's fear that he "wasn't ready for marriage." It was his support group that interrogated him through the breaking of his engagement and helped him to see that he was running away from responsibility, making Carla only another statistic of his search for pleasure without responsibility. Dan's healing will be a process, but the prognosis is good when he yearns to bring fidelity and pleasure together in his marriage.

DAMAGED BONDING

In wrapping up this chapter I will identify in brief scenarios some of the booby traps which damage men. If men's secrets are ever revealed, the majority of them will include painful and deforming experiences which parallel or supplement these:

Instrumental sex. Males are more vulnerable to separating sex from relationships than are females. As you reflect on the reasons I offered for this in chapters 1 and 4, let these stories help you to better understand. If you don't struggle with such problems, may these testimonies help you to reach out to damaged and frightened men who may still be unhealed victims.

Ron, four years into marriage, is still unable to resist occasional visits to massage parlors where explicit sexual services are offered and adult bookstores where repugnant homosexual acts are done to him. I asked Ron to write up a complete history of anything remotely related to his present sexual misadventures which threaten to destroy his marriage. A likely root event showed up at age nine. Ron's older brother permitted Ron to hang out with him and his friends. One day the older boys, in their early teens, were excited because one of them had arranged for his girlfriend to visit while the boys were on the premises. The guys carefully rigged a "privacy corner" for the couple, but tiny peep holes were cut in the blanket that surrounded the corner of the basement. The older boy successfully talked his girlfriend into the spot and into removing her clothes for him. The row of onlookers were perched on the other side of the blanket. One of them, at the first sign of forbidden flesh, laughed. The girl abruptly adjusted her clothes and ran out of the house. The event was regarded as hilarious by the whole gang.

"What connection do you see between that show, and your fascination with pornography and sexual encounters with strangers?" I asked Ron.

"Well, we were using her and didn't give any thought to what humiliation she might have felt. We did it for kicks."

"Exactly. And you are still doing it for kicks," I noted.

If Ron is to find healing he will have to take intentional steps to bring sexual pleasure exclusively into the intimacy of marriage. He is making a bold first step by telling the truth about his sexual past among trusted long-term friends. I serve as host, but he brings his support system with him. We are establishing reward and affirmation for Ron in exchange for his bold adventures toward truth and integrity. We will soon be working with his wife as he comes home to an intimate marriage.

Masturbation devastation. During my early years of teaching, Mel walked in for an informal appointment. "I am a senior," he began. "I graduate in two months. I transferred here from Gordon-Conwell and you don't know me. I've never had a class with you, but I've watched you. I think I can trust you. If I don't get one thing under control, I'm not going to be able to make it in ministry. And since I don't expect to ever see you after I leave here, I'm willing to tell you about it."

"Of course, you can talk," I said. "But I need to warn you that when people suffer together they may be stuck with each other for the rest of their lives. You may not be able to simply walk away from me if I have bled with you."

I recently asked Mel whether he remembered that opening exchange at our first meeting. When I recited it for him, he shook his head. "I was so frightened that I'm afraid it was all blacked out. I had never taken my life in my hands like that before, and I thought you might do violence to me somehow."

Mel unfolded a story of persistent masturbation. No, his wife knew nothing of it, and she wouldn't be able to deal with the truth if he told her. Yes, it was at least daily in frequency. It happened whenever he was alone after his wife left for work or if he went back to the apartment for lunch.

I had my class notes from Boyd McCandless' lectures on the "male and female sex systems" from my study at Indiana University on adolescent development. he had used the term "hydraulic system" in describing the powerful sexual appetite—not a drive!—that most males develop. But I had not tracked down his documentation. So I bought time with Mel and promised to get him some information to help him deal with his appetite turned compulsive. The summary of what I told Mel is found in the section *The Sex Systems* in a chapter called "Adolescence: Is There Life After Puberty?" in my *Bonding: Relationships in the Image of God*. I assured Mel that we needed to break out of the habituated pattern, and immediately we needed to lift his sagging spirits. At that time I did not realize that a mild depression associated with his "wife at work, husband in school" syndrome often expresses itself in secret masturbation.

"She'll have to know at some point," I said, "that you are defrauding her. All of your sexual energy belongs to her. But I'll help get you ready for that," I assured Mel. Self-hatred and low self-esteem are terrible tyrants. The cycles of compulsive behavior are all driven by motors of deeper and darker self-contempt. I took Mel into one of the very first campus groups I ever met with, though the men there never knew Mel's secret problem.

Within a few years, when I interrupted him at his pastoral office adjacent to a college, I found the waiting room nicely populated with people waiting their turn for appointments. You might guess what they come to talk about. I warned Mel that when he had passed through the dark days of dealing with his compulsive masturbation there would be a sign written on his forehead: Mel Can Help You! But it is only legible to those who are passing through a dark cloud very like the one he had survived.

Operation rescue. Since men are "fixers," and problem-solvers, always ready to help their women, a strange mixture of pity, affection, and sexual intimacy occasionally shows up. A pastor may indulge in pity while listening to a woman describe her terrible marriage, recent divorce, and lifelong yearning for someone to love her. He may find chords inside singing out, "Save her. Be the best lover she ever had. She deserves you."

I caution both men and women in ministry to avoid the pity trap. "There is one Saviour, and that's enough," I preach. "Don't imagine that you can solve everybody's problem or be everything they need. But you can be the facilitator. You can put them in touch with resources in heaven and on earth. Just don't try to be a savior." I am equally adamant in squashing the heresy that pastors are "married" to the church. I often say, "The church has one husband: Jesus. That's enough. We can't have bigamy scandalizing the church. Be the husband of one wife, the wife of one husband, and Jesus will affirm you for it, but don't go flirting with His bride."

I was moving quickly past the seminary bookstore one morning. The printer was running for me fifty feet down the corridor, so I stopped to check my mail.

"Dr. Joy!" a student hailed me. I turned around, only to be stopped a second time. "Are you Dr. Joy?"

"I don't know you, though," I responded, walking toward a distinguished looking customer emerging from the bookstore.

"I'm Bill Miller. I practice law in Florence, Kentucky. I was in the area, so I stopped to buy some of your books. I'm glad to meet you."

Attorney Miller took six copies of *Re-bonding: Preventing and Restoring Damaged Relationships* from the shopping bag and asked, "Would you mind autographing these? If I had had this book three years ago I think I could have saved my marriage. I was unfaithful to my wife, and I thought I was promiscuous. But when I read *Re-bonding*, I was amazed to see that I was an adulterer and that I really could be cured.

"Now I give a copy of *Re-bonding* to anybody who asks me to help them get a divorce. I've given away quite a pile of books to people, and it is cutting back on the number of divorce cases I work on."

Dan, whose story I tell in *Bonding*, found himself torn between his wife and a second woman. Eventually, his wife ended the marriage, unable to share her husband with another woman. It was Dan who shocked me into the reality that promiscuity (what the *King James Bible* calls "fornication") and double-bonding (what the KJV calls adultery) are very different disorders.

Both Bill and Dan were "tournament males" when I met them. It is likely Dan continues in his pattern of rescue and love. These competitive males, rarely vulnerable or able to tell the truth about their own needs, see themselves as competing for intimacy. If they provide well they deserve intimacy. If a woman seems relatively

Bonding for Life

secure and able to care for herself, the tournament male will often be unfaithful. His first line of justification upon being found out tends to be, "But you didn't need me, and she did."

When Bill Miller described his adultery I detected a complicating symptom, so I picked up a copy of *Bonding* and read the definition of "tournament species" in the animal and bird kingdoms. They are easily identified by their crowns, colored feathers, or their combative antlers and horns. "You don't have the plumage or the rack of the wild kingdom, but you have money, prestige, and power. You are accustomed to ruling wherever you roam. The whole industrial world bows down before you. And if you want to be generous with a secretary whose husband has abandoned her, you have a right to do that. If she is lonely, you have the right to comfort her. You call the shots."

A few weeks later Bill called. "I have good news. My former wife has agreed to come with me if I can get an appointment." Seated in my office with her, Bill pulled a copy of *Bonding* from my shelf and read to his former wife his own sexual "obituary" from the "tournament species" section. In those animal and bird species, males gather harems—as many females as they can win and support—and compete against other males by using status, courtship rituals, and sheer power to gather their cluster. In humans, both males and females, that impulse occasionally surfaces and nourishes the idea that they deserve all of the partners they can win—and they want to keep them all. Then Bill closed the book and said, "I want to be through with that part of my life."

In the next chapter we will look in detail at the tournament male, who enjoys a highly visible profile in our culture. In this chapter I have sought to establish the base for lifelong exclusive bonding. With that vision in place, we must explore more of the "unfinished business" we discover in helping men to make peace with their pasts.

THE COMPETITIVE TOURNAMENT MALE

For a dozen years I have planned and led backpacking adventures on the Applachian Trail in Virginia and, more recently, on the Sheltowee Trace in Eastern Kentucky. They appear as part of a basic course in youth ministry called "Discipleship Development through Trail Camping." Since about six years ago, we have added annual bike trips with similar objectives.

On these camping trips, we set out to equip seminary students with management skills and supervised ministry experience with teens in camping/community environments. As Daryl Smith and I laid out one week of parallel camping experiences, we found that with just a little alteration we could "merge" the two adventures for one overnight at Koomer Ridge—the Hilton of our campsites in the northern section of the Daniel Boone National Forest in eastern Kentucky.

Daryl would bring in twenty-four bike campers in three trail families of eight to join my backpackers—five families of eight. Each of these families consisted of

The Competitive Tournament Male

three seminarians and five teens. We had two women's trail families in our backpacking group. The bikers were all males. Roger Howell, of the Youth for Christ street ministry in Cincinnati, shuddered when we revealed our merger plan. He was bringing eight bikers and was himself biking with Daryl's troupe. But we ignored Roger's caution that there could be a bad scene.

The backpackers were well settled in at Koomer Ridge primitive campsite, and the meal preparation was done by the time the bikers arrived. As soon as the bikers' feet hit the gravel there was a charged atmosphere that all of us sensed. For two days three of the bikers had been speculating about the fact that there would be "chicks" on Thursday night.

Females, in street talk, rarely get the dignity of straightforward names from the mouths of competitive tournament males or their first cousins, "macho" males. I had added a rule to the basic orientation, only a couple of years before, when I heard the comment, "Hey! I hear there are going to be some broads on this trip."

"There are no broads on this trip," I announced in my coolest seminary professor manner. "But there will be a few young women with us. If I ever hear a slang name used by any of you, I will want to discuss the matching name we could call you." Our rule since then has been, "Address everybody with respect, and avoid sarcasm and put-downs of any kind."

This season we had moved through a week of all kinds of stress with no incident of cheap-shot-name-calling. But at Koomer Ridge there was a scuffle. The bikes had not even been properly stowed before the gravel flew. From out of nowhere a knife blade flashed and drew blood from the shoulder of a competitor. The battle was over turf rights to strut and win the attention of the young women scattered through the crowd of backpackers.

There is still another example. Seminary intramural athletes report that player behavior changes when women students walk into the bleachers in the middle of a game. Since the spectators are few at intramural games, it is easy to see anyone entering the field. Even the women notice it. Some of the men become recklessly aggressive, more active, and more vocal.

Anyone can speculate about why some males slip into a display mode when there are women present. Anthropologist Melvin Konner offers some provocative speculations in a chapter entitled "Lust," from *The Tangled Wing: Biological Constraints on the Human Spirit*. The book is both sensitive and shocking. In it he describes the behavior of tournament species animals and birds. Konner reports, for example, that 4 percent of the competitive bulls in a herd of elephant seals will impregnate more than 85 percent of the females in the herd. In such a tournament species the males will weigh up to seven times the average weight of the females. Breeding rights are won by persistent violence against other males. Indeed, among tournament species across the animal and bird kingdoms there are an amazing and illuminating series of common characteristics. Consistently in these male-dominated species:

(1) Males are fiercely competitive for breeding rights, with a flamboyant display of visible "sex markings" such as highly ornamental color, tufts of feathers, or antlers used in fighting and defending turf.

(2) Males are polygynous. They have an open number of females in each mating season, depending on successful competition and on the availability of an adequate food supply to support the harem.

(3) Males form a hierarchical structure, with the most powerful and successful males both controlling their harems of females and competing for herd status.

(4) Males have a low investment in the care of the young, and in some species seem intent on destroying the newborns.

In my *Bonding: Relationships in the Image of God* I go on to discuss the amazing characteristics of the non-tournament species. Konner's descriptions are at least a parable to instruct us about patterns in human pair behavior. The "perfectly bonding" species of animals and birds are exclusively monogamous, often mating for life and surviving alone after the loss of the original partner. They are nonhierarchical in their pair behavior and do not run in hierarchically organized herds. They move toward mating through a long and elaborate pair bonding ritual, with nest building completed before breeding. Then they share the care of the young, some males even having a capability to feed which matches the mother's natural feeding resources.

MALE DOMINANCE

When human males control and abuse their women and children it is inevitable that we would look for some way of explaining such behavior. The Marquis de Sade is said to have figured it out this way: "Since human males are larger and more powerful than females, it therefore is clear that they should control their women." We have coined a word to describe violent assaulting behavior by a powerful person upon a weaker person: sadism.

George Gilder, in his recently released *Men and Marriage,* describes another equally secular theory. Men need women to care for them, bear their young, and feed them. So men enter into sexual contracts with women by which they gather the food (or money) in exchange for the protective home, hearth, and sexual privileges the women can furnish.

The Judeo-Christian doctrine of Creation and Fall offers yet another theory. Man and woman were formed out of the original Adam. They were granted dominion as co-regents and joint-heirs of the promise. But two differing kinds of moral failure separated them, the woman was deceived by the serpent, and the man rebelled knowingly against the directions of the Creator. So two kinds of consequences fell upon them.

The woman was predicted to have complicated problems in all of her primary relationships. She would be the victim of increased complications and pain in childbirth. She would "desire" to control her husband, but he would retaliate by unilaterally controlling her—"He will rule over you" (Gen. 3:16).

The man was predicted to become absorbed in his work. His frustration would mount as he tried in vain to subdue the material universe. The silence about his awareness of need for significant relationships is interesting. Lastly, he takes away his wife's regal name, co-regent, and replaces it with a name for functional property, "Eve—the baby maker."

Within the space of three chapters in Genesis the idyllic vision of "two becoming one" is shattered. Emerging is a male who will dominate Eve and her sisters, indeed a harem of women, across millennia. Jesus counters this vision with His exclusive pair bonding summons to one man and one woman to be "joined together, let no one separate" (Matt. 19:6, my translation).

CONTROLLED BY INSECURITY?

Why would any man have his eye on a harem of women? Ben shared with his support group how at thirteen he was stunned by his best friend. Ben already had a vision of one exclusive, lifelong lover whom he would find and marry. But a friend confided to him one day, "I can't imagine living my whole life and having sex with just one girl." Ben was speechless, unable to comprehend how any boy his age could think that way. Ben's young friend may have been a witness to his parents' infidelity, and if his father was openly pursuing other women, the boy was a good learner.

Indeed, when a young man grows up seeing girls as "objects" for his satisfaction, visually or genitally, the universal effects of original sin are in motion as "competition, greed, and acquisition, even hoarding." A collection of "trophy" women as "sexual conquests" nicely fulfills that original sin desire. In our culture, as in many worldwide cultures, the promiscuous, "on the make" competitive male is viewed as "normal," even attractive in his demeanor.

For example, Phyllis George in doing a halftime interview with Dallas Cowboy quarterback Roger Staubach, asked him point blank, "How do you feel when you compare yourself with Joe Namath who is so sexually active and has a different woman on his arm every time we see him?"

Roger, as cool on camera as in the pocket of Tom Landry's "shotgun" offense, retorted, "Well, I'm sure I'm as sexually active as Joe. The difference is that all of mine is with one woman."

Here is another factor to consider. Is male competition for female attention driven by low self-esteem and insecurity? Are such men hollow, or simply filled with worries that drive them to a competitive mating style of keeping their options open?

Low self-esteem may, indeed, masquerade itself as high self-esteem. Arrogance does characterize many of these competitive, polygynous, tournament men. They leave the child care and child rearing to the wife. "Woman's work," they call it. Control of income and wealth is exclusively their domain, and often it is collected and banked secretly, or just as secretly squandered. Since low self-esteem is a universal human trait, every male is vulnerable to buying into the tournament model of sexual animal.

The payoff, however, more often than not, is devastating to these "I did it my way" tournament men. They tend to devastate their more monogamously programmed women, but in any culture which respects the value of women, they will find themselves having, not only the devil to pay, but their women and children as well.

BENEVOLENT DICTATOR?

When "on the make," the tournament male is able to move through all of the right steps in forming a courtship or pair-bond. They even make the appropriate exclusive promises and follow through by making every effort to keep their multiple mistresses from having contact with each other. I recall a famous Dallas millionaire who managed to rear two families miles apart. Only his will identified the second family as his own as well.

The tournament male is Don Juan to the rescue for a woman in trouble. He will literally fight off her other suitors. Indeed, he loves to win his women through combat of sword or wits. Today's male most often does this through a show of money and power. The so called marks of mid-life crisis in males, following teenage fads, and purchasing coveted possessions are most often signals of a reawakening tournament instinct.

Since the secret life of the competitive-tournament male is sometimes more complicated than honest living, the tournament husband tends to accelerate his high-control patterns. When he is pursuing or actually controlling and supporting more than one woman he is likely to seem happier, have higher energy, and be more sexual with his women than when he is stagnant and not in a "winning streak." In contrast, a more monogamously oriented male will cease being sexual with his spouse when he is pursuing her replacement. In his adultery, he is at least "faithful" to his preferred lover.

The competitive-tournament male tends to supplement his amorous courting behavior with threats and violence to make it clear who is going to "rule the roost." Complicate his stress with alcohol or drug consumption, and it is anybody's guess where his need to control may take him or where his violence may strike.

FALLEN DESTINY?

It is easier to document the formation of the "macho" male than the more prevalent "tournament" male. Chapters 7 and 8 describe how damaged adolescents become self-protecting and fragile macho adults. But the "tournament" deformity seems deeper and nearly universal among human males. Melvin Konner's and George Gilder's theories may be universalized. However, I take seriously the idea that original sin has deformed us all.

In his chapter on "Lust," Melvin Konner reports that 85 percent of animal and bird species are either nonbonding or polygynous tournament species dominated by larger and clearly marked males. He goes on, almost without noticing the parallel, to describe human male sexual behavior. The same percentage of human males tend, at some time or another, to experiment with trying to attract and hold multiple females. In many human cultures today, and in most human cultures across time, males have traditionally supported harems of women.

George Gilder argues that the male determines to find a safe place to produce offspring and to keep his options open. His argument sees the male as relatively weak, highly insecure, and dependent on a resourceful and faithful female.

But the Scriptures describe the Eden sin as fracturing the bond, trust, and mutual respect that existed between the male and female (Ish and Ishah) who together form the image of God. The sin which "smashed the Adam" emotionally and spiritually, ushered them into a nuclear winter of broken relationships. While the woman was renamed "Baby-maker Eve" to denote her indentured function, the arrogant Adam, taking the racial name for himself alone, regards the whole creation as his property. He will name and control the whole thing—including the renaming of the woman.

The curse and consequences of Genesis 3 make it clear that males think about relationships differently than females. He is preoccupied with things. He will work, sweat, produce, putter, and be frustrated by his tools and his playthings, but relationships rarely seem to enter his picture, except to analyze them and reduce them to their "function." Hence, Eve—Babymaker! Polygyny is implicit in this refocusing of woman's role. She is no longer lover and peer, but an object. And if her function determines her value, then woe is the woman if she is barren.

There is hope for healing from the tragic effects of the Fall. As with other effects—the complications and pain of childbirth, for example—it will take intentional confrontation to make a difference. Doing what comes naturally will consistently tend toward male dominance, even violence. Transformation will come only by intentional choice, by open repentance and apology, and by daily consistent practice of respect for women. This will cultivate the exclusive bond and bring the spouse back to her place as joint heir of God's grace and co-regent in the creative management of the household and of Planet Earth. All of this is wonderfully predicted by Joel and Peter, both of whom present this communication as the word of the Lord, "In the last days, God says, I will pour out My Spirit on all people. Your sons and daughters will prophesy" (Joel 2:28; Acts 2:17).

MARITAL RISK

Combining the nearly universal deformity of the competitive-tournament male with the damaged macho variety we will look at in chapters 7 and 8, it is clear for women that entering into a relationship with any man is a considerable risk. It is reasonable, therefore, to end this chapter with a list of cautions. They might be considered as bottom line truth in advertising statements. I offer them more as appeals to invite us to finish our business. And if our friends and lovers will help us to articulate the truth, the damaging demons will be largely disarmed. Together, we can surely be the instruments of each others' confession, repentance, and transformation.

1.) *Beware extravagant displays of power.* The guy with the hot car who prowls the parking lots at high school is exhibiting tournament muscle. The glamorous adult male who "displays" through extravagant clothing and the parading of playthings such as vehicles and stereos is likely dangerous. These tournament males tend to be seen in "full regalia"; they hide behind closed doors when they are "unpresentable" for any reason. Remember this image: The tournament pheasant cock with extravagant display of brightly colored feathers, compared to the drab and plainly-dressed female, is out to collect a harem.

2.) *Beware the rescuer.* The tenderest of the tournament males are likely to "display" by their caregiving. They are at their best when they can "fix" something for a woman. This may be an emotional hurt or a flat tire. Their worth seems linked to their ability to rescue and to "deliver." One version of the rescue is purely financial. Are you broke? Women beware. He will bail you out. Are you poor, he will bring gifts to your children. The woman is forbidden to reciprocate; if there is any giving to be done, he will be the giver—except for sexual favors. And in these favors he sees himself most often as "providing her the real love she never has had." Thrown off balance by his gifts and financial extravagance in her behalf, she feels she must compensate and sees the sexual favors as her "payoff" of the debt she is accummulating in meals, gifts, rent and car payments, and general inappropriate extravagance.

A monogamous male times his giving impulses to the growing seriousness of a relationship. His generosity may be enormous, but it will be released with discretion to avoid the impression that he is buying favors. Men must realize that the bail-out strategy is a poor foundation for relationships. Men who marry after bailing a lover out cannot discriminate between acts of charity and those of love. Those who fail to break free will begin a pattern of rescuing other women for most of their adult lives. If the women they love ever become strong, stable, and competent, these men will search out another in need. Their cry echoes, "She needs me more than you do." He loves to be needed. He's a rescuer.

In this chapter I have described a central vulnerability in many men. The very thing that makes so many of us attractive to women is our competitive and tournament behavior. It is our seeming glory and certain downfall. We are lonely and scared. We need help from others to move on.

SEVEN

TOUGHENING
THE MACHO MAN

L ance had the look of the Marlboro man, with the three-day stubble of *Miami Vice's* Don Johnson and cowboy boots that have recently been up to the ankle in stuff "where the buffalo roam." Like a cool ladies' man cruising in a Playboy world, honestly out to have everything his way, Lance does not hide his sexual exploits. He brags about his current "live in" as if he is inviting the whole world to copy his lifestyle. He is determined to call the shots to his own advantage, and let everybody look out for themselves. I hadn't seen Lance since he was in high school, but I recognized him turning forty and graying.

"I'm really glad to see you. Are you doing okay?" I probed directly, but warmly. My vocation in pastoral care has always moved best on the street with the occasional probe that could be direct without being explicit—to the point of probable human hurt.

But Lance's grin preceded my invitation to candor. He responded, "I'm great. Everything is going my way."

Unfinished Business

Lance's style had successfully isolated him from most every human being in five counties. He had driven his wife out ten years before. It took a little longer for his son's family and a daughter to write off any possibility of maintaining a relationship with their father. I had learned that he was now reduced to a hermitage—surviving alone fifteen miles from the nearest town. The "live in" was a weekend arrangement he was currently enjoying 150 miles away, and none of us ever saw her. "Everything is going my way," said it all.

The macho facade is a thin disguise of toughness that many men wear to protect themselves from others discovering what empty and hurting people they really are. Those who have concluded that they have a "zero" value, create an attractive but largely hollow image to hide behind. Looked at through a medical metaphor, the tough and cocky male is an artist of self-protection hiding behind emotional scar tissue. We may never learn what orginally caused the wounds. But there is one thing Lance and men like him learn from experience: *never be vulnerable again.* The scar tissue serves as protection to prevent people from getting too close and knowing too much. They are afraid that another deadly wound of rejection would follow such knowledge. The scar also serves to mask the painful reality of low self-esteem. When the macho male does offer gestures of intimacy in what appears to be a healthy relationship, he usually keeps other relational options open as insurance against being dumped.

Such Casanovas also end relationships abruptly, leaving friends, lovers, fiancées, and even spouses behind. It doesn't take an X ray of their emotions to read shame, fear, and desperation in the guys who keep the sleeping bag rolled up behind the girl's couch, because they know they cannot establish an enduring, trusting, lifelong relationship. "I'll call," he says as he prepares to leave. But he never does. He knows when he is through, but his scarred emotions don't allow him to be honest with her.

He has to be the one to "dump" his partner. It would hurt too badly to go through a healthy ending of a relationship. Casanova is reflexively programmed to protect his deformity. One more blow, he fears, might kill him.

When I had my conversation with Lance, the macho facade was still an enigma to me. It took two of my students to identify and take apart the construction of the fragile but effective mask. The building blocks of the macho facade seem to emerge in the following sequence:

1. Early destruction of the male self-esteem;
2. Making a decision to build a wall to survive;
3. Developing a self-protection strategy to guard the damaged, hollow person;
4. Using anger energy to define relationships;
5. Sabotaging potential intimate relationships out of fear that the real, deformed self will be uncovered.

DESTRUCTION OF SELF-ESTEEM

The macho scar usually begins with some devastating wound. Typically, it is formed to protect against a previous pain or loss. Lance was always number two in a family of two sons. Constantly compared to his brother, he always came up short, the object of criticism, correction, punishment, and abuse. A desperate mother would occasionally talk of sending Lance to the White's Institute where they handled rebellious boys. These experiences sent Lance down the macho path.

I learned more of the typical macho character during a three-way conversation with two students who described their descent into that attitude and their later success in shedding its scars.

Jon, youngest of three children, was the "little victim" in a divorce. Feeling abandoned by his natural father, and with his mother absorbed and troubled in a new marriage, Jon saw his stepfather as indifferent to him. While a teenage brother and sister turned to alcohol, sex, and drugs for affirmation, Jon had no such outlet and felt abandoned.

I had never met Jon until a Saturday morning campus seminar on developing healthy relationships brought us together. For that seminar I developed the lifelong time line you saw in chapter 4. As we began our review of the "World of Abnormal Relationships and Perceptions," I suggested that everyone close their eyes and recall the most painful memory of childhood.

Jon told me that when he closed his eyes, he could see himself standing at the top of a cold, metal-edged stair rail in a two story inner-city house:

"I'm sure it isn't true, but in my memory, I can't remember my mother ever coming to the floor where our bedrooms were. I remember night after night standing at that cold and lonely spot begging Mother to come upstairs and tuck me in bed. I wanted her to hug me and hold me. But she would tell me to go to bed, that I was old enough to do that by myself. I can still feel the pain of crawling into bed and sobbing for what seemed like hours, until I cried myself to sleep. I now know that she was having trouble in her new marriage, but I couldn't understand that. I was just a child!"

Jeff's erosion of self-esteem was more subtle than Jon's of feeling loved. Jeff's father, a popular high school gym teacher, was friendly to everyone in the community, and especially to teens. So as Jeff grew up, he knew he needed to excel in sports to gain his father's favor. From childhood, his dad was his worst critic. Though Jeff excelled as an athlete, his father offered little positive feedback, reserving his praise for Jeff's peers. Jeff's dad would privately criticize his performance. Such humiliation was delivered to the older siblings as well. By the end of high school, Jeff was running on empty, carried a heavy countenance, and was set to strike the macho pose.

The concept, "self-esteem," is poorly named, because there is almost no contribution the self can make to esteem. A sense of worth is derived from significant relationships, interaction, and the feedback which affirms the person. Lance received violent and negative ingredients added to his "cup of self-esteem," and he was set by the teen years to begin acting out his destructive pattern of behavior. Jon was drained of any sense of intrinsic worth, but his was less violent than Lance's experience. Jon experienced emotional bankruptcy as a vacuum was created around him when he really needed to be hugged, kissed, and supported. Jeff was caught in a double bind of being regarded as lucky to have such an affirming father, but nobody knew how shabbily his dad treated him at home.

DECISION TO SURVIVE: SELF-PROTECTION

The visible toughness of the macho male is a clue to his early decision to make it alone. The "macho scar" I am describing turns out to be only a tough mask. The scarred male usually will be crippled in his efforts to establish respect, vulnerability, or intimacy in relationships so long as the core issue of negative self-esteem remains sealed away and undisclosed. He may go through the motions of intimacy, especially sexually, but in his self-protection armor he cannot be open and vulnerable to further risk or hurt. Instead, he simply uses women as instruments of his own desire and tends to abandon them quickly when the threat of intimacy encroaches.

The bottom line is the human need to survive. Abraham Maslow has defined it as the controlling need. In a life-threatening situation, the need to stay alive takes priority over everything else. So it is not surprising that abused children, such as Lance, most often make a decision to cope—to learn to live in spite of impossible conditions of rejection, emotional deprivation, and physical violence. Infant mortality and disease cases are sometimes symptoms that a child has given up fighting against the odds. But Lance was a tough little survivor, so he plugged his ears and steeled himself against his mother's persistent emotional and physical abuse.

Jon, sobbing in the night, gritted his teeth against his mother's emotional abandonment, loss of his natural father through divorce, and isolation from his older siblings. He now grieves, "The three of us kids all tried to cope for ourselves alone. We didn't pull together. We could have survived without so much damage—and I suffered the least of the three—if we had only helped each other. Instead, we were each shattered in our own way. Crying in the night, I remember promising myself that I would be such a good boy that they would have to love me. I would succeed at everything I did, so they would have to applaud me. They'd see! I was going to be good at everything I did!"

Jeff, observing his popular father turn into a depressed and bitter husband and parent, sided with his mother, made friends with her in her own emotional anguish, and came to resent his father. He determined to survive, but had to leave the first path to manhood since his father's rejection blocked the way to simple father adoration. Jeff's decision to survive was complicated. He reckoned, "To be a man, I must be more like the man my mother deserves." It was a long road because he had to build his manhood prematurely, foreclosing part of his youth, and do it without the benefit of a positive relationship with the man everybody else admired.

ANGER: SETTING BOUNDARIES IN RELATIONSHIPS

Remember that the macho personality begins with the destruction of self-esteem, leaving the young boy or teenager feeling empty. Among those who grow up coping there is a universal core commitment to survival. So it is not surprising that most of these macho kids have told themselves that there were other people to blame for their pain. Such deep and growing resentment tends to replace the self-esteem ingredient until the inner cup is full of anger.

Jon said, "Suddenly, I realized that I had survived by protecting myself from being hurt by others. Never again would I be vulnerable. I would bump early and give the signal that you're not going to hurt me, so keep your distance. I would expose a little piece of my anger very early in friendships, so they would know not to mess with me. This survival strategy became a fifteen year rehearsal of deformed social skills that have kept me from ever letting anybody really know me."

It is typical that the macho facade man will come on strong, make a bid for attention, attract friends who admire strength, and seek to be in control. Such a facade is especially attractive to a woman who has been victimized by men in the past. Her damaged self-esteem responds almost magnetically to the macho way. In some cases, her cry seems to be for protection by a strong man. In others, she seems drawn to a damaged man against whom she can bounce her own unfinished business, resentment, and anger. But the final alliance is frequently between the macho man and the damaged woman, and the hurts they sustained early in life are perpetuated in the future.

I remember meeting another handsome macho guy, this time on a Christian college campus. He made an appointment with me after hearing my convocation address on the signs of a promiscuous man. My appointment roster was full that day. I had offered a path back to wholeness. "Is there life after promiscuity?" I had asked in my address.

"Do you want to know what the young men look like?" I asked after setting the agenda for examining the sexually damaged people on campus. "Do not imagine that they are aggressive and dangerous. On the inside they are hollow men. The mildly macho look is a thin facade by which they try to convince themselves that they are tough, independent, and in need of nothing. But there are so many of them that the image of the macho man has become the poster image of late twentieth-century America."

There were more than 2,000 students and I was planted in the middle of one side of a wide auditorium. Gorgeous young adults were stretched a full 180 degrees from my left to right side. "Right now," I said, "if these hurting guys are in this auditorium, they want you to believe that they don't need anything, that they have it all together. To make this point they will pretend to be indifferent to everything. They will spread this morning's sports page across their lap and defy the speaker to get through to them. Don't take them seriously about this 'cool' posturing. They give themselves away in their masks of humor, small talk, mild obscenities, and unwillingness to sustain eye contact. And here, they attempt to disguise their feelings of emptiness, shame, and inferiority by hiding behind sunglasses, even in this indoor arena." My statements were only conjectures; I had seen no newspapers or sunglasses in the auditorium.

"How did you know me?" Rodney began our session.

"What do you mean?" I was baffled, and the convocation was now several hours past.

"When you described me. I folded my sports section, tilted my chair down from its hind legs, took off my sunglasses, and looked around me. Three of my friends were still buried in their morning papers. I thought, 'Thank God! At least I heard this guy. My buddies are still trying to look cool hiding behind their newspapers.' How did you know me?"

"The description found you because your name is 'Millions.' I've worked with a lot of guys who are tough on the outside, but they are wrecked and fragile on the inside, and they know it. When they start telling the truth, they are on their way to complete healing."

"Can you tell me how to get out of the empty syndrome you described? See, at age fifteen things were terrible at home, so I left in an angry fit of rage. I moved in with this woman twice my age and thought I was having everything my way. I felt loved, and the sexual experience was wonderful. But in three weeks she was tired of me, so she fixed me up with another woman, then another. By the time I was nineteen, I had slept with more than thirty women. Then suddenly I met Jesus and everything changed. I came to this Christian college to play football, and I thought that whole chapter of my life was ended. Now, this year, I've met the woman I really want to marry. She's a beautiful and godly woman, who has no history of sexual involvement in her relationships. And I haven't been sexual with her either. But Dr. Joy, not a week goes by that I don't sleep around on her. I cheat on her all the time and I can't get it stopped. It's killing me. Can you help me?"

There it was again—the rage building toward the parents, the leaving home. The experience of being used by an older woman turned on into a series of sexual encounters that emptied his sense of worth. Now, Rodney's question to me was the open door to his return to wholeness: "It's killing me. Can you help me?"

SABOTAGE: THE SELF-DESTRUCT STRATEGY

Rodney's voluntary confessional appointment was a rare move for a man with a macho facade. Indeed that initiative means that the facade is breaking away. More typically, the facade is carefully maintained. "I don't need that stuff!" or "Maybe other guys are empty, but not me!" are standard denial responses. For them, the relationship games go on. Several special strategies are practiced.

1. *The arm's length seduction.* The macho male is the master of tremendous first impressions. Singles' bars abound with these introductions. They are meant to bait and titillate. An honest relationship is the last thing on the macho man's mind. Instead, he goes for the party, for the hype, for the entertainment blitz, even for the one-night stand in a sexual encounter. If they do move that far, the arm's length behavior is endlessly and artfully executed. The affair goes through the gestures of intimacy, but no attachment occurs. If it does begin to form and

vulnerability emerges, the macho facade sends another message: escape. Don't call me. I'll call you, is a typical farewell.

He leaves one-night stands and brief romantic escapades with a promise to be in touch. This rarely occurs because maintenance of the facade demands that he shuck off this close brush with vulnerability and move into safer encounters. In a very brief time, the facade scar thickens and self-protection desensitizes the original vision of vulnerability and intimacy. He quickly develops compensating strategies for getting sexual contact, even if it must be without permanence and lifelong commitment. He becomes skilled in using the tricks of seduction. He can tell a dozen or a hundred women, "I never loved anybody like I love you." Without intending to lie, he has become a compulsive con artist. He has fallen into regularly rehearsed scenarios in which "use and abandonment" are practiced with finesse and skill. Our hollow man is moving on a one-way road into the ultimate isolation.

At one level, the machismo's friends and lovers are often ready to do him violence. But at another level, it is important to remember the loneliness and isolation he experiences if we cannot bring him to integrity and honesty. We can gain insight into his character by noting what Robert Coles and Geoffrey Stokes found in their *Rolling Stone* survey. They observed that young males who lose their first love tend to grieve longer than the young female partners. This original and tender vision of an exclusive lifelong relationship, when exploded, may simply hurt so much that the macho facade is rolled into place as a denial mechanism. This denial is an essential anesthetic for continuing through the magnetic social patterns which promise sexual expression sooner or later. And for the macho man, it is almost always "sooner," because he protects himself against his own vulnerability to love. He can execute the sexual transaction for simple animal pleasure, and depart emotionally unscathed in an arm's length seduction.

2. *The bump back approach.* In virtually every relationship, the scarred macho man keeps his options open by keeping distance. It is no mystery that women who have encountered such a man often suffer a devastating loss of self-esteem. Even if she was whole and healthy when she fell into his arms, she later finds herself bumped back, reduced to an emotional wreck. And if she neglects to get her sense of wellness back, and strays into the singles scene, she is likely to be an even more striking target than before for other predator males. Indeed, Aldonza's cynical lines from *Man of La Mancha* are the wail of many women who have tangled with the macho facade: "One pair of arms is like another! They're all the same!" Devastated by his exploitation, her self-respect has been reduced to match his own emptiness.

3. *Projecting self-contempt on others.* The macho's own low self-esteem often gets pitched in the face of friends and lovers. It is as if his cup of self-esteem is filled with mud. He has plugged the emotional wells which might have welcomed genuine intimacy. Obscenities, accusations of infidelity, and hostile assaults tell you what is inside the speaker more than anything else. Jesus once said, "Out of the abundance of the heart the mouth speaks" (Matt. 12:34). So if the affective center of life is full of junk, the mouth is going to spew it all over the place. It is important to listen with one ear toward Jesus. Remember that the scarred man is dying on the inside, and wants real intimacy more than anything in the world. But he has developed a strategy by which he at the same time:

1. Protects his damaged self-esteem by keeping friends, especially women, at arm's length;

2. Deliberately sabotages the relationship while blaming others for being inadequate, unworthy, or imperfect in some trivial way;

3. In all probability, he has also developed a compensatory strategy by which he has already established an-

other option to which he can turn, secure in knowing he has devastated the other person first, and has avoided being dumped.

In this chapter I have presented what I have learned from others about the development of the macho scar. They have shown you the high cost of those self-protecting strategies. Their stories differ from those of millions of men hardened by early or late experiences, in that they chose not to live out their lives in splendid isolation. They told their saga to another.

The truth is a man may marry, have a good relationship, be reasonably faithful at a technical level, and be dying on the inside. If he has few friends, cannot laugh at himself, and seems edgy or defensive on a regular basis, you can be sure he is hiding something. He is dying of isolation.

The tough and lonely stag image of the human male is a signal for grieving. Even in those species where competitive breeding necessarily isolates the powerful and solitary male, such loneliness is a mark of a fallen and broken universe. But it is intolerable in the human community where the first principle is that "it is not good for the human to be alone." Solitary confinement, the prison system's penultimate punishment, is a Siberian exile experience, whether we are in a family, a marriage, or a community.

EIGHT

DISSOLVING
THE MACHO FACADE

I grew up among scarred and insecure boys who were abusive, distant, and threatening to their less damaged peers. By the time I was in college I was no longer afraid of them, and a few of them even shared their unfinished business with me. Indeed, I was elected president of my college student body in a sometimes rowdy political campaign. My campaign was engineered by the tough and cool guys on campus. I suspect now that I was the only outsider who knew their feelings of helplessness and inadequacy. One by one these guys, some of them recently returned from World War II, would pour out their stories to me. Their fierce loyalty got me elected over the "Mr. Nice Guy" supported by the incumbent campus leaders, college faculty, and administration. For reasons which I cannot unscramble, these campus toughs trusted me with confidential reports on their past and present troubles. I connected some of them to Jesus in profound and transforming conversions. I am discovering through a round of fortieth anniversary reunions that many of these once insecure and compensatory males are today my distinguished friends in highly effective careers. Most are honest men, no longer plagued by the fears that haunted their younger years.

But not until past my sixtieth birthday did I begin to unravel the actual interior structure of the macho facade. I did this through the help of the two students I introduced in chapter 7. The young seminarians, whose journeys were quite unknown to each other, were members of the same weekly "formation" group with me. This chapter will be built around their description of the lonely world of self-protection. You will discover how they made the frightening entry into the world of vulnerability, which is essential for establishing the integrity and intimacy that males in the third decade of life need so desperately.

LOCATING AND LOVING THE LITTLE BOY

Jeff: "I think I made a breakthrough this afternoon talking with my roommate. Woody is a special and faithful friend. When he offered to talk to Lucy, I knew I could trust him. So he went to tell her that I needed to be away from the relationship for a while, that I was working on some things. I feel so sorry for Lucy, because I just can't shake my negative reactions. And although we are going to be married in six weeks, more and more I just want to run away.

"Woody asked me to describe what had happened over the weekend when Lucy and I went to her home in Tennessee. So I told him. It was a little thing, but Lucy scolded me for something I was doing as we were riding in her dad's new pickup. I went silent. I just shut down. I wanted to leave. I always seem to want to run away. It must be my special strategy for coping with feelings of shame and worthlessness. Lucy complains about that— suddenly I will clam up and cut everything short and just go away. And she's right. That's what I do.

"So as I was describing all of this to Woody, I said the

strangest thing, 'But I was just a little kid.' I couldn't believe my ears. Here I was describing what had happened last weekend. I am twenty-three years old. Yet that's what I said—like I was going crazy or something. I'm a full-grown man, and I said, 'I'm just a little kid.'

"I called this kind of a breakthrough, because talking with Woody, I suddenly saw something—the way I coped with my dad's abuse when I was young. I would leave the house. Or, I would grab things for overnight and go stay with my grandparents who lived nearby. I'm still trying to run away, and I'm a full-grown man. I went through fifteen roommates, and mangled several quality relationships while I was in college, but I still have this flight impulse. I abandon people instead of risking being hurt again."

PRESCRIPTION FOR HEALING

Don: "It's the little boy in you that wants to run away, but your commitment to Lucy and your clear perception of her as a worthy person make you know you want to marry her. You seem to have a scared little boy in you as well as a competent and basically healthy adult."

Jeff: "That's it. But I can't get the two separated, and the scared little boy takes over."

Don: "I once referred a student to Dr. Poole, a psychiatrist in Lexington, who helped him to cope with episodes of emotional abuse in his childhood. Will's mother frequently punished him by locking him in his bedroom. He couldn't get out, and he would panic. Later, his interpersonal relationships showed traces of a compulsive clinging for security, evidently out of fear of being punished or abandoned. One day when Will was very depressed he stopped by my office. He seemed dangerously depressed, so I phoned Dr. Poole and reported what I was seeing and suggested that Will might need medication to be stabilized. The doctor phoned the Wilmore drugstore, and Will went to pick up the medication. He was back in twenty minutes to show me the label. Dr. Poole had prescribed the medication for Willy, not for William or Will. We laughed together in a wonderful moment of insight. It was the little boy's fear that needed the treatment.

Jeff: "I notice that I always identify with the underdog in movies and on television. It is like there is this little Jeff inside me who shrivels up when anything goes wrong or someone gives negative feedback. Little Jeff feels like he can never do anything right, and he wants to run away when things go wrong. He feels helpless and worthless."

Don: "But the adult Jeff that I know is a reliable, productive person—always on time with assignments, radiantly handsome, and calm."

Jeff: "I know. That is the way I really am, except when something drops me back into my little Jeff."

Don: "Will you let me give you permission to comfort little Jeff? It would mean that it is okay to say to him that whatever he is feeling is all right. You would never have made it to adulthood if he hadn't learned to cope by running away from the abuse. But now you're going to take care of him. You won't let anything bad happen to him.

"You can tell Lucy that you are working on little Jeff's fears and hurts, but that it is not her problem. You are okay as a man. Tell her you want the little boy to find healing, so you can be a playful and healthy adult."

Jeff: "When I feel afraid and vulnerable, how can I keep little Jeff separate from my own adult self?"

Don: "Try nurturing the frightened and damaged little boy. Hold your pillow in your arms and cry at night, comforting little Jeff. Thank him for taking good care of himself and doing what he knew he had to do to survive. You'll bring healing to him and the reflexive emotional flashbacks will leave you. What you are doing is grieving. A good grief always takes a long time, but it is worth it because it brings healing, wholeness, and integrity. I know you as a tender, sensitive, and gracious adult. I know that you needed a different kind of parenting than you got, especially from your critical and abusive father. What he did might have worked well with another kid, but it was painful and damaging to you. So welcome to the world of your own healing."

RECOGNIZING THE MACHO SYMPTOMS

One profoundly insecure man I counseled described the engagement proposal he made on his third date with a woman. "I knew I had messed up past relationships because I got both more defensive and offensive as friendships extended across a few weeks. So, I said to myself, 'You're twenty-nine, and it's time to marry. This is the woman you should marry.' I swung my car around in the middle of a two-lane highway and went back and asked her to marry me, even though I realized the proposal would ruin this relationship too."

Jeff's situation was not so drastic, but he did find himself damaging his engagement. He told how his engagement almost ended when he resorted to bickering with and criticizing his fiancée. When he finally succeeded in offending her, she would strike back with words that drove him down into depression and self-annihilating abandonment.

"Slowly, I began to see that I was imitating how my father treated my mother. I hated the way he treated her, yet here I was doing the same thing. It was ironic that I had rejected that way of relating, yet I seemed doomed to repeat it."

Jeff, entirely alone, was able to recognize and report his discovery about his macho damage. Jon, in contrast, had been "doing his own surgery" in our family room, in great agony. An amazing moment exploded in my office during a spiritual formation group lunch. Jeff began to give us the play-by-play account of his solitary break-through. Jon's eyes widened and he shot a knowing glance to me across the room, then blurted out his own exactly parallel story. When Jeff finished describing the shabby treatment he was giving his fiancée, Jon illustrated how he was taking out his unfinished anger against his mother and dumping it on Arla.

"The closer I got to Arla, the worse I treated her," he complained. "I can't believe how negative I was. In my mind I would criticize her for everything. I would tear her apart inside my head—worried that she dressed too provocatively. I even questioned her spiritual maturity. She was too emotional and not logical enough. Everything about her seemed to bother me. Me, for pity's sake, with all of my junk and failures. Who was I to be criticizing her?"

DISSOLVING THE FACADE
Working with Jon across a six-month period in reconstructing his interior "little boy" damage showed me an X-ray image of the macho facade. And the most telling line came through his tears.

"This is such a familiar territory to me. I have been using my own hurt ever since I was a little boy. It hurt when people didn't meet my needs. I determined to keep people far enough away so that I couldn't ever be hurt again as I was in growing up and crying myself to sleep."

Jon told how he had successfully sabotaged dozens of friendships, and two or three prize romantic possibilities. "I was skilled at using mildly offensive strategies, often masked in humor, to put people on their guard. It was as if I had found a way to keep them off-balance, so if the relationship turned sour, I could walk away and blame it on them. I was so fragile I knew I couldn't bear to hurt anymore, so I kept my dukes up and bumped them away."

Jon's breakthrough ushered in a season of grieving for the "bump back" strategy he had used for the last sixteen years. He took the time to walk through an inventory of faithful friends he had "bumped" so he could protect himself and walk away with no emotional risks.

TO LOVE, OR NOT?

Don: "Jeff, you're so gentle, you sneaked up on us in the formation group Tuesday. Nobody was prepared for the bomb you dropped. You should see Jon work on this stuff. He perspires. Twice Robbie and I have seen him reduced to what looked like involuntary muscular seizures as he appears to wrestle with himself. How did you work through dissolving your self-protection?"

Jeff: "That was the Tuesday after the weekend I had worked through some real struggles with Lucy. I was finding that I could not open myself up to anybody— even to Lucy—in a deep way. So that week we went out to eat on Thursday. I told her, 'I don't know what's wrong. I know it's not you. There's something I've got to break through.' I had come to this point in relationships before, when I would start finding things wrong with the person. I'd say to myself, 'This is close enough. I can't handle this,' Then I would go on into another relationship.

"I told you I went through fifteen roommates in college. I would soon find something wrong with each of them. I wouldn't let them get close to me, and I would not want to get too close to them. But I never realized what was happening until my relationship with Lucy. I was going to have to be vulnerable to Lucy or break the relationship. It was almost as if I was trying to criticize her enough to push her away."

Don: "What was it that you saw you had to break through?"

Jeff: "It was my terrible fear of being hurt—rejected— by somebody if I let them too close to me. I didn't trust Lucy. I think I saw that it was my fear that created the barrier. To be sure I wouldn't be the one hurt, I would begin criticizing and keep her from getting close. It was my way of avoiding hurt."

Jon: "Wow. Just last summer I stepped out on Arla to keep an option open in case she dumped me. How sick! All I was doing was playing games that guaranteed to keep me from getting close to anybody."

Jeff: "I can understand that. What helped me get through this was my commitment to Lucy. My feelings were totally out of the picture by this time. I operated on a decision I made to break the intimacy barrier."

Don: "What was the commitment made of if the feelings were gone?"

Jeff: "It was a commitment to working through whatever was damaging our relationship. I strongly sensed that God wanted us to be together. So I decided I simply had to learn to trust her."

Don: "By this time you were engaged, weren't you? How did you work through the lack of trust—the fear of vulnerability?"

Jeff: "I sat in my room all weekend. I prayed. I asked Lucy for some time away—to be alone to objectively look at our relationship somehow. I started reading Dr. Larry Crabb's book, *Inside Out*."

Don: "What changed in your perception of yourself during that weekend? Anything?"

Jeff: "When I say I didn't have the capacity to love Lucy, I mean that all I was seeing was negative stuff, and I felt like that's not love, at least not by the definitions in 1 Corinthians 13."

Don: "Did it ever occur to you, Jeff, that this negative material might be coming out of your feelings about yourself? See, when I first met you, you were struggling with feelings of agnosticism. You said you couldn't pray. You felt worthless. Yet, neither you nor Jon looks like a candidate for low self-esteem. You are both good looking and intelligent individuals. So I never would have thought to ask about deep feelings of hunger for worth, self-respect, competency, and confidence. In fact, you may remember that I asked about your relationship with your father, since that is such a crucial predictor of problems with religious belief.

"Men with unfinished business with their fathers tend to flirt with total agnosticism about God or at least to experience 'prayer paralysis.' This was my hunch when you first came to me to talk about your inability to pray. You see, if your Dad is rejecting you, he is the 'image of God' to you, and that is enough to shut down your praying, because it says you aren't worth listening to. It is low self-esteem of the most personal and spiritual sort. I wasn't surprised to see that same low sense of self-worth damaging your relationship with friends and now with Lucy.

"See, if you were down on yourself, you would reflect that negativism onto your closest relationships. If you feel worthless, you will need to bring the other person down to the same level."

Jon: "That's interesting. Unbelievable, what a perspective!"

Jeff: "I think the breakthrough was learning that God truly did love me."

CAN LOVE BE REAL?

Jon: "How in the world am I going to be able to love Arla? I'm not a good lover. I'm not healthy, Jeff. And I hear you saying the same thing about your relationship to Lucy."

Don: "What does a good lover do?"

Jon: "A good lover focuses on strengths and encourages the person. I said originally that I needed her or enjoyed her, but love her? Loving means if she gets burned and her face is scarred, I am going to be with her. Right now, I know Arla loves me and I wonder if that's why I love her? Do I just love her back?

"I just want to be sure I've got the right kind of love to make this work, because I've never loved before. I've never given my heart to someone before, never been committed to loving anyone before."

Don: "Let me remind you guys that you are the resident authorities on the macho syndrome. The one characteristic of the syndrome you have been defining is the inability to be truly vulnerable, to risk loving even when exposed to the threat of being hurt.

"There is another characteristic that I see now and then. These kinds of males tend to be competitive, falling into the pattern of the imperfectly bonding male."

I describe the tournament male in chapter 6. These showy and competitive men tend to develop harems—all at once, or one at a time if they can't get away with polygny. They are always "looking," constantly trying to figure out how to attract and support additional females. This is true in the animal kingdom as well as among humans. These males have wandering eyes. Instead of investing the enormous energy it takes to live honestly and vulnerably with one woman, they live superficially. They try to minimize their risks by secretly maintaining multiple relationships. But the tournament male inevitably becomes the legendary lonely and solitary male.

Jon: "Does that change the roles, then, for a human male, if he repudiates being a tournament type?"

Don: "It means that we've got to put down our fallen nature. All males are fallen—sons of Adam! It calls for a high investment in the care of the young. It means that the sacrificial husband who lays down his life for his wife is going against the grain of human nature."

Jon: "What does it mean for a man to lay down his life for his wife?"

Don: "Well, it means, at least, you're always vulnerable. Everything is at risk."

Jeff: "Always vulnerable. Wow."

Don: "You can see what that will do for you. It means you have to be intentional. Intimacy is the name of this marriage. You don't have any secrets to hide. There is nothing you could not own, because you have built unconditional trust in this relationship. You lay down everything."

Jeff: "That's scary, though. Do you know how scary that is for the first-timer?"

Don: "But you are already finding out how rewarding it is."

Jeff: "Yeah. I've never felt better now that I've decided to break down the wall."

Don: "And it will only get better."

Jeff: "But what if the old fears come back and I feel like running away, maybe after we are married?"

Don: "They will return. You can count on that, but you have broken the power of those old fears. Now you can take Lucy with you and revisit the old experiences. This is a sort of retroactive healing, as you walk down painful memories with someone who knows, understands, and loves you."

SORTING OUT SELFISHNESS FROM GENUINE CONCERN

Jon: "I've got this selfish, self-righteous something inside of me. I'm doing great because I'm doing such a good job of getting healed. It's frustrating. Isn't that sad that I'm so self-centered?"

Don: "Wow. Sure, Jon's doing it."

Jon: "Isn't that sad that I think that way? It's pathetic."

Don: "But you told us recently that on numerous occasions, in class or during chapel, you've been so overwhelmed by peace and love that your eyes have filled with tears. You are simply celebrating God's faithfulness to you. When you acknowledge Him, you know then that you are not riding on your own self-will or resting on your own goodness."

Jon: "Then I get so humbled. How can I go from so much love, and so much respect for Arla, to suspecting that it's all emotions and not real? I say to myself, 'Let's get this straight, Jon! We're talking fifty years here, and you better be sure on this one.' I struggle between going back into my negativism and what is legitimate questioning and responsibility."

Don: "Those are likely the reasons why our culture developed the pre-engagement and engagement stages. During that time a couple can make a responsible evaluation. You can sort out your feelings about engagement, marriage, family, and the rest of your life."

ONE PATH TO WHOLENESS

In reviewing, we see the unfolding pattern of the macho facade as a strategy calculated to help the man survive. Thus, we can understand that the key to dissolving the attractive macho mask requires working backward through the same sequence of four steps. Remember the four steps involved:

1. Destruction of your self-esteem.
2. Your tough decision to survive.
3. Your anger-driven boundary setting.
4. Your self-destruction sabotaging of relationships.

The best path to recovery that I have observed requires beginning with the last step and climbing up to the final repair of self-esteem. It looks, then, like this:

1. Acknowledge that you are your own worst enemy. Your strategies of "self protection" are isolating you and starving you to death for honesty, trust, and intimacy in any relationship. This "confession" is the toughest of all of the steps of recovery and transformation, because it means admitting that your survival strategy which has "worked" for you is also destroying you. I told Jon one night during a painful surgical session, "You likely wouldn't have made it if you hadn't hardened your heart to people. It was your survival strategy. But it is what is now turning you into a lonely man. It is time to let the strategy go."

2. Defuse the "anger" explosives with which you "bumped back and protected yourself" from people who could hurt you. See whether you can go back to a primary "stressor" from whom you protected yourself as the earliest means of survival.

Recently for one man, who was unable to write well enough to ventilate his lifelong resentment, I offered to interview him on microphone. We then made a cassette tape book, which we called "The Story of My Early Life." The book of tapes became his permanent record of the abuse and humiliation he endured in his childhood.

3. Decide to be vulnerable again, now that you have

Dissolving the Macho Facade

managed to survive an emotional holocaust. Own your feelings of anger or inferiority that have fueled the macho self-protection. Name it as a "self-protecting" strategy. "It is my problem, not yours!" is a good beginning line in a genuine apology for sabotaging a friendship. If the first rule is that "feelings are okay," then the second rule must follow quickly: "It is my junk, I am responsible for dumping on you." You cannot be a friend or love another until you are friends with yourself. You can love others only to the extent that you love yourself.

The Jesus axiom is deadly as well as wonderful. It is a terrible thing to "love your neighbor as yourself" if you are running on empty, packed with emotional mud where self-esteem should have filled the cup. If you are desperate, violent, and a saboteur of relationships, then others will certainly wish that you would not "love" them too much!

4. Refill the cup of self-esteem. Separate out the "little boy," the "wounded child," or the "devastated teenager" in you from the present man of integrity you are in accepting God's transforming grace. Tell the little boy, for example, "You did a good job. You were just a child and it was not your fault that bad things happened to you. You are a survivor. So it's OK to hurt, to cry, and to scream. But I am here now to protect you, and I've got wisdom and energy now to guarantee that you are safe. So let me take care of you." If your memories are more visual than verbal, let your memory take you back to the most painful memory of your devastated period of life. Frame that picture as if you were looking at it on TV, watching the humiliation and the heroics you performed to survive. While that image is at maximum power, create another parallel picture of you *as you are now*, with your present wisdom, integrity, and ability to cope with that long-past tragic episode still on your other "screen" in memory. Go one step further and say, "If I could revisit the scene, this is what I would say, do, and feel as

I delivered that young boy out of the jaws of humiliation and destruction." As this healthy and mature image dominates, you will have "separated" your childhood from your present. And, wonderful reality, you will be equipping yourself to be God's agent of deliverance for other helpless people as they are being exploited, abandoned, or abused.

Give yourself permission, too, to accept the feedback, the affection, and the unconditional positive regard that comes from other people who know your whole story and steadily value you. You are now refilling your cup of self-esteem with the most precious and indestructible fuel for healthy behavior known on earth—you are loved!

For those of us who care about men's unfinished business, the hardest part is often to accept their statement that "the problem is my own, not yours." But to find healing, they will need faithful friends and spouses, not "rescuers." The macho facade must be abolished by the man himself. We can affirm our unwavering commitment, but the work must be done by the man.

In this chapter, you have listened to two recovering macho men. As a subset of the larger species of tournament males, they may have revealed some symptoms that help you to understand yourself or someone of importance to you. Most of all, the bold honesty of Jon and Jeff is a model for all of us who long to be people of integrity in the outer world and who are willing to go "inside out."

NINE

MEN AND MARITAL FAILURE

W ill I die?"

We faced the question several times with our young son Mike between the ages of three and six. If he experienced the pain of a finger caught in the door, or saw the blood from an accidental gash in his arm he would typically ask, "Will I die?"

Our assurances were calm. We wondered where the question came from, but didn't have to wait. He volunteered easily, "I want to grow up to be a daddy."

In early childhood, boys rarely have a sense of how one shows his marks of maturity and responsibility. They are not aware of the trajectory of attraction, love, marriage, and parenthood. Only the final vision of parenthood was driving Mike: "I want to grow up to be a daddy!"

THE VISION: GOOD NEWS

Evidently the urge toward maturity, marriage, and parenthood is strong in all healthy humans when the family matrix is secure and stable. Since the sex-role markers of marriage and parenthood are so central to the core of personhood, any failure in those areas of mature harvest can be devastating.

With the risks involved for men and marriage, this is the good news: no marriage will be lost unless there is a bonding failure. When I refer to *bonding*, I am using the word as a shorthand term to include all of the mysteries by which two people become attached to each other. Both bonding formation and maintenance depend upon virtual daily, significant contact of eyes, voice, and touch. So the health of a marriage or parent-child relationship may be viewed in these very public ways that people deal with each other.

I am glad to announce this good news to all aspiring and enthralled lovers. I have found that nothing can destroy a marriage—financial problems, sexual problems, infidelity, an incestuous childhood, or workaholism—if a powerful bond has formed which can bring both partners through turbulence back to integrity.

But the footnote to good news is bad news. Every healthy bond is constantly under assault. Terrible crosscurrents rage in our culture threatening our most treasured relationships every day. And the bottom line can be the worst news of all. We sometimes are so damaged that we develop a "lover's amnesia." We deny that we were ever in love, and we distance ourselves from the truth about how much time we have invested. Our sense of loss might be deadly. Amnesia and denial save our sanity and sometimes our lives.

In this chapter, I will create four vignettes reporting the myriad reasons for marital failure. As complicated as the reasons are, marriages can be saved if the bonding is right, or if it is healed and made right. This holds true even for marriages which were founded on deformed or inadequate bonding. These stories are actually composites of cases I have worked with from each presenting problem.

Men and Marital Failure

A CLASSIC SET OF FOUR CASES

The Jacksons. Helen came to ask whether, as a Christian, she would be justified in divorcing Richard, her husband of twenty-two years. They had no physical contact in the last five years, and now she found deep feelings stirring inside as a divorcé at work began to talk to her. She asked, "Could I divorce, then remarry and repent? I wouldn't want to give up my faith in the process."

The Carltons. Theresa hasn't trusted Bob since six months into their ten years of marriage. Bob had been sexually active with other high school girls, but when he took her to bed when she was only fourteen, he said she was the only one for him—forever. Then at age eighteen, six months into the marriage and pregnant, she discovered that Bob had been sexually involved with three of her friends while engaged to her. Now, coming in at daylight after his company Christmas party, she accuses him for the last time of still another infidelity. Enough is enough, Theresa thinks, so she packs her things and moves back to her parents' home with the three children.

The Knights. Gene listened to my description of sexual addiction and its roots in the *King James Bible's* use of "fornication." "I saw myself in the addiction cycle," he said. Then he unraveled a history that began with dipping into the *Playboy* centerfold images at age fifteen. At eighteen, he made his first visit to an adult bookstore. There he found a video booth that came equipped with actual sexual services that shocked and repulsed him. Still he has been going back now for seven years. He has been checked twice for AIDS. He is turned off by his wife. She complains that they never make love. He is both scared and ashamed. He still is active at church and hopes his bookstore visits are never detected. But he knows he is hooked; he is a sexual addict.

The Smiths. "What's going on with me?" Dale wonders. He has a good marriage—better than any he knows of—yet he found himself deeply attracted to Susan, a colleague in his law office. So at an annual convention, they shared a hotel room for three days. "It doesn't take anything away from my wife Joan," he told himself. But now he feels bonded to both women. "How can that be?" he wonders.

BONDING: THE "EPOXY GLUE" IN MARRIAGE

Creation provides amazing lessons, especially when viewed through the lens we call zoology. People who study the pair-bonding patterns of the warm-blooded Creation species command our attention. They report, among other things, that some species are so fiercely and exclusively monogamous that if a mate dies, they never re-mate, and live out a solitary existence. These are the *perfectly bonding* species and include golden eagles, marmoset monkeys, ring doves, coyotes, and wolves, among others. But biologists and anthropolgists agree, that while humans are distinctly monogamous, we are an *imperfectly bonding* species. That is, we are attracted to the idea of one, exclusive lifelong bond, but we are vulnerable to distraction by seductive environments or relationships.

In humans, the quality of the bond and its durability seems to be related to two things over which God has intentionally given us choice and control:

1. Slow and exclusive development of the bond with careful postponement of genital contact until the full bonding foundation has been built and ripened. To be "naked ... and not ashamed" denotes full knowledge and familiarity between the pair, with no mistrust and no inhibition.

2. Daily maintenance of the exclusive bond by recapitulating its steps that initially took months or years to develop. These pair-bonding steps include:
- Visual scanning of the partner.
- Voice contact—both trivial and substantial.
- Eye-to-eye contact and communication.
- Nonsexual touching, especially hands and face.

- Face-to-face rituals of communication and kissing.
- Full body contact, especially skin stroking.
- Genital intimacy.

The perfect marital bond is one which is forged (1) slowly, (2) exclusively, and (3) by synchronizing sexual pleasure with full adult responsibility. It is not surprising that an "alien bond" can form across the same sequence. Successful infidelity follows the same bonding patterns. All that is required is an investment of time, opportunity for privacy, and the unfolding sequence of gestures and attachment.

When sexual pleasure, for example, precedes legal marriage, the appetite for genital excitement is almost inevitably forged into a "sex without responsibility" pattern. The partners will be highly vulnerable to seeking out sex with no strings attached. The stolen fruit of teenage sex typically brings a harvest of affairs outside of marriage, except in the rare case when the exclusively intimate couple quickly makes it to the church and guards the intimacy in absolute confidentiality. When there have been partners other than the spouse, a new bond may be formed only by establishing complete integrity through full candor and repentance face-to-face. Such honesty can provide a base on which future accountability and careful discretionary checkpoints are established to maintain the honest foundation, so painfully restored.

The best news of all about bonding is this: when it is right it is virtually indestructible. Contrast the deformed appetites of "sex without responsibility" to the happy bonding that is exclusive and timely. Here, restraint holds off the passions of young love. The engagement period and the wedding, which bring the avalanche of full adult responsibility converging in a marvelous crescendo for the young lovers, permanently fuse full adult responsibility with sexual excitement. These couples find their sexual bond carrying them through sickness, bankruptcy, grief, and the child-rearing and launching years in great style. Their sexual pleasure was married to the full spectrum of adult responsibility. Fidelity is their middle name, and they cannot imagine casual sex because they know it would be impossible to live in such a fantasy. Such unreality would seem so silly—attempting intimacy with a virtual stranger for whom no lifetime of mutual responsibility was even remotely probable. They are not vulnerable to the fantasy machine seduction of the culture. Their minds are fixed in a reality that is "too good to be true," but is grounded in a long-term fidelity base of sexual and personal fulfillment.

Families, armed with these realities, frequently look more to the quality of the young bonding couple's relationship than at their age or financial resources. Such families are eager to spread the tribal largess to undergird the newly forming household, launching an indestructibly forged marital bond. Parents who trivialize young love frequently live to suffer the consequences of sexually active teenagers who grow up to move through a series of marriages, spawning children who will grow up without the bonded protection of their natural parents.

COMING BACK FROM AN ENDANGERED MARRIAGE

Take the four vignettes with which I began this chapter. Let them stand as examples of the worst things that happen to break down marriages. If my basic thesis stands, then we should expect that attention to the quality of the marital bond and its maintenance will outweigh the most tragic interruption of marital fidelity.

Jacksons. When a marriage is "frozen," it is not uncommon for all touching to end. The couple may still sleep together, but they avoid physical contact. Typically, conversations are carried out without the benefit of eye-to-eye contact. Bonding is put in reverse. If there are twelve steps to bonded intimacy, then there must be a back staircase by which intimacy dies. Perhaps there are a dozen corresponding "de-bonding" steps.

Men and Marital Failure

In Helen's case, the shutdown occurred when she objected to the merely mechanical sexual contact in which she and her husband engaged. She felt used. Richard, unwilling to be a beggar in any sort of sexual game, simply said, "Then I won't ask again. We are good people and we cannot even consider divorce, but I can live without sex." And they had kept their bargain for five years. But with each passing day, they were vulnerable to new adventures of the heart, and Helen was the first to feel the quickening of her affections. At work she met a man who understood her and wanted to marry her. The feelings she thought were dead suddenly came alive. She was eager to know whether she would be justified in divorcing Richard in order to marry and be loved again.

I played off the options for her. It was easy to predict some of the effects of leaving her marriage to marry the divorcé. Her own integrity would be in jeopardy. Effects on her children were easy to predict should the marriage end. When I suggested working with her as a coach to create a new marriage with Richard, she was skeptical. I challenged her, "The first thing you will have to do is end the relationship at work. We'll not be able to get a fresh bond going with your husband until you turn your heart away from that new friendship making your bonding energy exclusively available for your husband."

"And," I said, "I want to see Richard."

I outlined a series of steps which were calculated to rejuvenate the original marital bond. Within a week, Helen was being overwhelmed with deep feelings of attachment and attraction for her husband. Eventually Richard phoned and asked me to coach as he worked on his side of rebuilding the marriage.

COMPULSIVE PROMISCUITY: THE LONG ROAD HOME

Carltons. Bob's "first love" was lost before it became genital. Indeed the bond with that first love has hovered over all of his promiscuity. As he tells his story, it is clear that his quick intercourse with the next girlfriend was "compensatory." He was getting even with himself for not taking the first true love to bed. So that relationship was flawed, as were all of those to follow. Theresa, he admits, was "number seven." And his bonding glue is virtually gone. He had three one-night-stand affairs with Theresa's friends during their engagement, and has had five more affairs outside of the marriage.

Genital contact without marriage tends to shatter the core of integrity in the partners, though the "first-time" partner is likely to point back to this as the original, lifelong dream bond. When sexual pleasure is ripped loose from full adult responsibility for the consequences of the intimacy, a deep shattering occurs. Many of these promiscuous people, with their shattered core of personality and self-respect, are able to make the promises of fidelity and, indeed, may appear to be exclusive and faithful to an unmarried lover. Should they marry, however, some mysterious trigger of mistrust seems to be pulled in both partners. Their past irresponsible sexual practices evidently turns a virus of mistrust loose between them. Theresa has accused Bob of dozens of affairs. Indeed, her lack of trust has likely pushed him further into promiscuity than he would have gone if she had blindly trusted him and his faithfulness to her.

You can see that Bob and Theresa have further to go in repairing their marital trouble than the Smiths with their one case of adultery. Multiple partners extending before and into the marriage are sure signals of severely damaged self-respect—they are projecting their own feelings of insecurity on each other. Bob is simply using other partners as if they were disposable women, echoing his exact feelings of being a zero.

Where promiscuity is present, the cure requires internal healing at the core of personality. I used to talk about *reparenting* such people. Now I am delighted with the new findings about healing for compulsive disorders. These include the sexual addict. We commonly find this

Men and Marital Failure

deep damage associated with catalytic environments such as child abuse, alcoholism in a parent, and authoritarianism in the family of origin. But we also find the compulsive damage in people who have strayed into a single catalytic episode, from which they came away sensing a loss of integrity and feeling worthless. They typically have a whole arsenal of self-depreciating labels with which they describe their feelings about themselves.

Healing for the promiscuous requires something deeper than dealing with sexual problems. And that healing requires special grace administered in a healing community. Typically a confidential support group of three to six people, to whom the entire history of failure is disclosed, is just the right environment in which complete healing can take place. But the time frame requires from one to three years of high investment. The group provides the healing, forgiving, and reconstructing foundation. The grace of Jesus is the agent for the change, but people must do again for the person what parents do for young children: provide tangible feedback that fills the tank of self-respect, based on significant, unconditionally affirming relationships.

Only healthy people can develop healthy intimacy, so the rebonding must be postponed for promiscuous people. "We need a celibacy club," one man told me at a singles' retreat in a great church. "The worst thing we can do is to try to date, because so many of us are damaged. The first thing we do is jump in bed."

I asked what the club would look like. He asserted instantly, "We need a medallion to hang around our necks that tells everybody: 'I need people, but I am not ready for a relationship.'"

When the support network has done its healing work, and when accountability is firmly established with people who hold them in unconditional positive regard, the Carltons will be ready to begin reconstructing their marriage as healthy people. A wife almost always falls into a *symbiotic enabler syndrome* in which she becomes a part of the problem rather than a part of the healing. With outside help, such as a support and healing community, a wife can be set free to remain steady during the rehabilitation process.

The worst of all predictions for marital survival are those marriages decimated by promiscuity. Indeed, when Jesus states the "exception clause" in His divorce teaching (Matt. 5:32), He holds out the flame of hope for all marriages—"saving for the cause of fornication." You may be surprised if you take the time to track down all biblical statements about fornication. Check the *King James Version* for the complete listing. More recent translations tend to have lost for us the Bible's consistent use of fornication to denote promiscuous, sexually addictive behaviors.

The *New International Version*, for example, translates fornication as "marital unfaithfulness" in spite of the fact that "adultery" is already in the text and describes the effect of remarriage by a violated and abandoned lover. For example, see Matthew 5:32 and 9:19. The concepts of promiscuity and adultery are clearly and consistently used in Scripture. Look at Proverbs 6:26, for example, and see how clearly the adultery and promiscuity effects are contrasted: "The fornicator [promiscuous person] reduces you to a loaf of bread; The adulterer [alien bonder!] stalks your very life" (my translation).

Knights. Robin and Gene are suffering the tragic effects of Gene's addiction to pornography and the sexual payoff of the adult bookstore scene. There is a very close connection between what the Bible calls fornication and what we call pornography today. You can see *porneia,* the New Testament root word from which we get fornication, in the English word "porn-ography" better than you can see it in fornication. The same shift in developing the English language brought *picus* into English as "fish."

Men and Marital Failure

In the adult bookstore, Gene has been exposed to dozens of different male service contacts across several years. The terms promiscuity and fornication, as used in Scripture, consistently refer to these deformed affective disorders. When Gene the fornicator turned himself in to me, I outlined the way to come back to wholeness and healing.

1. Write out a bold and fearless sexual history. Get it out on paper where you can control it instead of having it control you.

2. Share your story with at least three absolutely trusted people outside of your family, whose acceptance will confirm God's forgiveness. Utilize their help by contracting weekly accountability to them and emergency responses from them. When you are caught in a "hypnotic trance" and on the way into an addictive cycle again, call on them for support.

3. Maintain that accountability network for the rest of your life, and expect the reconstruction of your self-respect to take at least as many months as the number of years you invested in developing your compulsive addiction. In chapter 11, I outline my modification of the well-known "Twelve Steps" program, first used by Alcoholics Anonymous. I recommend it for any voluntary, confidential support group, including those which are formed for compulsive sexual addictions.

Since Gene's voluntary and open confession to me was clearly his first transformation of shame into healthy guilt, I gladly announced, on the authority of the words of Jesus in John 20, "You are forgiven. Now, go and tell your story to the network group and you will be whole." This is a long road to recovery, but the damage to self-esteem is so tragic that it must be carefully reconstructed to break the destructive addiction.

GRIEVING THE LOSSES: HEALING FOR ADULTERY

Smiths. Dale, attracted to Susan, a law partner, has found himself investing a lot of time, emotional energy, and, not surprisingly, sexual intimacy with her. Adultery has followed the same bonding pattern as Dale's original bond with Joan. Indeed, Joan recognized Dale's rising energy when she observed his contact with Susan over a period of several months. After all, Joan had been there when Dale's high-bonding capacity was first awakened toward her in engagement and then marriage. If Dale and Joan find their marriage surviving on scraps of time and energy, they will easily understand why most marriages ending in divorce fail because one of the partners becomes involved (bonded) with someone in the workplace. When at least forty hours a week are invested in a common work-setting, it is not surprising to see new but alien bonding relationships emerging.

There is a widely held myth that the biblical grounds for divorce is adultery. What most of us don't know, however, is that such a thing is *nowhere* taught in the Bible. Adultery was the biblical grounds for execution, not divorce. Execution was the penalty largely because the marital partner was regarded as property and adultery constituted the theft of the spouse. The criminal nature of such a theft remains as law in most states and is described as "alienation of affection." If we put aside the idea that a spouse is property, then adultery becomes a tragedy of a compromised relationship—a loss of exclusive, confidential, and shared experience. As an occasion for major grieving, adultery would then be regarded as a "fatal attraction" that might yet be dissolved and the original, precious bond salvaged.

In Jesus' day, it appears that no Jewish man was ever in danger of being charged with adultery. The male-dominated Jewish culture had seen to it that adultery was distinctly a woman's problem. The case of the woman caught in adultery, reported in John 8, borders on humor because she was apparently doing it all by herself. No participating male was dragged in for capital criminal charges, even though she was charged as being "in the very act." Josephus reports that Jewish males might have multiple wives simultaneously. They were even tolerated having access to prostitutes. The patriarchs seem to have impregnated every ovulating female in the household except their own daughters—this included multiple wives, concubines, and handmaidens. They were all regarded as the property of the male. The male owner had the power of life and death over his females. So adultery was a woman's fatal error, and the death penalty was the man's prerogative.[1]

But if the spouse is not property, then adultery is a signal of a failing marital bond. When Dale and Joan sat down to take stock of what happened, they saw the alien bonding pattern clearly. Dale then was faced with the awful choice of abandoning his alien bond, or accepting that he had killed his marriage. They were confronted with an important and painful question: What can we do to give top priority to our wounded relationship in terms of investing time and affection for restoring our bond and reestablishing trust? But Dale was facing a painful marketplace question. He asked, "How can I end my inappropriate bonding behavior with Susan, given my daily contact and opportunity to nurture that destructive sexual relationship?" A universal rule applies here: Once a relationship has moved to genital contact, it will not be terminated so long as access to privacy remains.

The tragic questions faced by Dale and Joan open the door on the intentional energy required to rejuvenate a wounded bond. It is clear that extreme measures must be taken to shut down the destructive force of the alien bond. Nowhere do we see the universal human vulnerability to alien bonding more clearly than in such care-based relationships. God has created us with a powerful bonding gift, but we are responsible for focusing that gift toward our exclusive, lifelong partner.

RE-BONDING FOR A DAMAGED MARRIAGE

The simplest rule to follow in bringing back a failing marriage is this: Do the basic bonding work again—now.

This means making intentional time for playing, talking, and touching with one another. You must make a priority of doing all of these every day. It requires an atmosphere of honesty and candor, sharing feelings of failure and inferiority. Indeed, without shared histories of failures and dreams, a marriage always remains a partnership of peers, not a one-person union. Talking, holding, touching, and hugging are the necessary modes of communicating while sharing deepest feelings, troublesome memories, and the present pains. These essentials sustain the dynamic bond which is ever forming and strengthening as it is nurtured day by day.

The simple rule of continuous bonding will "risk-proof" any marriage against outside invasion of an alien bond. The wonderful thing about being created human is that our basic need is for ultimate honesty in an exclusive relationship. "It is not good for the human to be alone" (Gen. 2:18, my translation) applies to all of us. This means that we are always searching for significant relationships. If the marital friendship and sexual bond are healthy, our monogamous tendency predicts that we will not be sitting ducks for an affair. But since we are human, we have an enormous capacity to reach out and touch other people. Such a magnetic pull can draw almost anyone into destructive intimacy.

These four painful cases of marital and bonding failure and their paths to wholeness are a reminder of how urgent it is for a man to make peace with his sexual history and energy. We are, indeed, "fearfully and wonderfully made" (Psalm 139:14), and this is from our "mother's womb." To be born male is to be charged with enormous sexual potential. Our sexuality is at once the primary definition of our identity: we are sons, brothers, boys, men, husbands, and fathers. But is is also the fuel which drives our creativity, our productivity, and our expansiveness—to revisit J.D. Unwin's studies in anthropology.

We live in a culture which desensitizes the privacy

and mystery of our sexuality and encourages us to exploit our basic needs. We are offered sexual stimulation without patient establishing of legitimate intimacy. We are offered "safe sex" in order to dull and destroy our capacity for exclusive bonding with one partner for a lifetime. And, since we are fallen human beings, we have little resistance to anything which appeals to pleasure, instant satisfaction, and apparent "safe" secrecy. So our sexual gift is at once our greatest source for happiness and our most vulnerable spot for emotional and moral bankruptcy. The way home is over a path of honesty, repentance, and rehabilitation. The next chapter goes in search of an integrity definition of "real manhood." Then a final resource chapter offers you a set of strategies for maintaining integrity and recovering it when it has been bruised and beaten along the badly marked path from childhood to adulthood.

Cultural pressure

CALLING THE "REAL MEN"

T hree things remain: (1) To grieve with men who have significant "unfinished business," (2) to celebrate men who have courageously faced their fears and found wholeness, and (3) to identify the visible, central marker of the truly healthy human male—a characteristic which consistently appears in men who rise to the full stature of manhood.

DAMAGED FATHERS, DAMAGED SONS

I remember Jim. At age fourteen he called to me as I walked the mile from work to home. He used my name—my first name, and the voice sang out with eagerness and friendship. I turned, walked up to him, shook his hand, and asked his name. "Jim Miller," he said. Across the years our voices connected occasionally, and the friendly nod or wave indicated we were "neighbors" of a sort.

A couple of years later I noticed a disturbing trend. He started to skip school and dropped out by the next semester. He worked on his car too much and frequently spent long evenings away from home.

One morning on my walk to work I was startled to hear the squeal of rubber at daylight as a Camaro headed off toward town. "What kid?" I thought. But looking, I discovered it was Jim's father "getting rubber" in the midst of a mid-life crisis, showing his symptoms behind the wheel.

In a year, Jim was convicted of a felony as he pounded the fast lane of compulsive hungers. In two, he was dead in uncertain circumstances. I grieved our loss. But the village was quieter in the night and slept easier with him gone. He was easily the handsomest young man we will produce, and he is gone.

You can see how pain is transmitted. Watch it in a John Bradshaw "five generation genogram" or catch his PBS series *On the Family.*¹ Or, if you want the horror straight, read it on your streets. When anyone sets up an idolatry and worships the wrong gods, the axiom comes true again: *The generations suffer!* Since the Bible always tells the truth, it is not surprising to find the universal reality there. But, as with the Ten Commandments, they are not true because they are in the Bible. They are in the Bible because they are true. No one can "break" God's universal laws; but any of us can break ourselves on those unchanging true realities if we ignore them.

I grieve for Jim, but I see him in a parade of damaged men across the generations. No doubt Jim's father is a victim too. The issue is never blame, but loss and grief. Look at the word of the Lord: "I the Lord your God am a jealous God, punishing the children for the sin of the fathers to the third and fourth generation of those who hate me" (Ex. 20:5, NIV). Jim's family, across the generations, are all going to be losers until some young man in some generation of "Millers" says, finally, "It is enough. This silliness of macho manhood with its idolatries of power, control, and cool facades must stop. I will be the last of the damaged sons." When that happens and the chain is broken, God's mercies are even more generously unleashed. If the built-in punishment for idolatry and "hatred" of God's ways with people seemed spread across too many generations, look at the longer lever of fidelity and honesty. Exodus 20:5 describes God's grace and mercy: "showing love to a thousand generations of those who love me and keep my commandments."[2]

SPILLED SEED AND RAGE

Monte put the moves on the freshman sorority sister. As a big senior he was fully practiced. Any standards about waiting for sex were eroded during his freshman year, so long ago, so many women back. But Betsy was stunning—the pick of the crop of new sorority women, and he knew how to deal with her early first reluctance.

"I'm pregnant," she confided three weeks into their relationship. "So what?" he reasoned, "as a senior, I'm ready." Entrepreneurial, ready to "branch" his parents' business, he was free. So they married.

The beautiful daughter seemed the perfect seal to their whirlwind romance and sudden marriage. So perfect that as Betsy crammed the remainder of her teacher's credentialing in with motherhood, and Monte launched his own business, the lovely Lucy seemed all they could ever want. At thirty, Monte urged Betsy to have her tubes tied to take the pressure off and to close the family with a single child.

Five years later, surviving a school bus accident, Lucy needed a quick blood transfusion. Monte and Betsy huddled in the waiting room outside the intensive care unit. Twelve-year-old Lucy was in danger.

"Let's try the mother first," the hematologist suggested. In a few minutes Betsy was back.

"It's obviously your type," the doctor said to Monte.

But with the lab work checked, the sentence that changed his life fell on Monte's ears: "Wrong type for you too. Is Lucy adopted?"

Calling the "Real Men"

Today, only Monte and Betsy know the truth. Betsy was pregnant, obviously, before that first rush Monte put on her. She knew it was a possibility. Betsy took the blame.

The hospital located the blood Lucy needed, but a dozen years later Betsy is still unforgiven. Monte refuses. His playboy years scattered his seed freely. The occasional abortion in his wake gave him only brief second thoughts.

"She's not my own flesh and blood," he complains, and Betsy drifts deeper into pits of shame and humiliation.

Self-pity and self-protection are the fuel of Monte's unrelenting grief. He is trapped by the humiliation that would follow on his own head if he abandoned Betsy and the truth came out. And Lucy is baffled at the sudden sullen change in her once exuberant Daddy. Blinded by his rage against Betsy's sin, he cannot own his own promiscuity and irresponsibility. Monte is trapped in a box canyon, walled in by arrogance, self-protection, denial, and pride. He is dying and killing off both Betsy and Lucy with him.

THE ANGER DANCE

The devastation of "It isn't fair!" rings out in everything Gerry is and does. His father died when he was two, so he has no memory of him. His stepfather abandoned his mother when he was eleven—just when Gerry's dad was his prized possession.

Now turning thirty and alone, incompetent in pursuit of a woman, Gerry defines every male friendship by the boundaries of his anger. He is racked by jealousy that everybody else had a "normal" childhood. Every acquaintance who befriends him hears the same wail. If there were an audience of thousands, perhaps, he could balance the injustice of the universe by accusing God and his fathers for their sins against him. But Gerry is the victim of his own unfinished boyhood, emotionally devastated adolescence, and anger that shut out the world of affection. "Curse God and die!" (Job 2:9) was the unhappy but desperate "comfort" of Job's wife. Gerry's friends border on such last-straw options when he envelops them with jealousy and neurotic manipulation, and leaves them no alternative but to pity him.

Having been denied a father, Gerry is now the center of a stress tornado which dances into people's lives. If they stick with him, Gerry demands that they must engage in his pity dance. He cannot collect and sustain a complete network of unconditionally committed friends. The dance is too exhausting.

NO KIDS ALLOWED

Jack, at nineteen was in love. But the relationship literally ended in bed. He and Evelyn developed a slow, intentional bond, but it went prematurely to intercourse. Once "turned on" sexually, Jack exercised a surprise option with Susie, a returning high school crush, home from college for the summer holiday. Back to Evelyn the next day he simultaneously impregnated her and infected her with the sexually transmitted disease that Susie gave him. Jack paced my floor allowing the crack in his developing armor to disclose a glimpse of light: "She's going to kill our baby," he complained. "Don't fathers have any influence on the decision?" I think it was the last instance in which I saw the beautiful potential Jack once carried. In her blind and understandable rage, everything was settled for Evelyn. Jack funded the abortion, even saw her through it, but the relationship was mortally wounded. It was too complicated, too painful, too humiliating.

Three "live-ins" later, Jack finds Judy his kind of woman. She is hard working, good looking, and *obedient*—a criterion for satisfying the sexual needs of Jack's hardening macho personality. But there is an impediment. Judy has a son from a previous marriage. Jack simply will not tolerate a child in his life. None. Now or ever. He cannot tolerate being around anybody's children. I suspect the "denial" hangs over from the abortion, and as the years pass, I know he studies children born in the year of his lost child—but keeps them at a safe distance. So after three years with Judy and her son, the relationship is winding down. There is an uneasy truce that may sustain the affair for a few more years. Judy furnishes the "nest and food." Jack furnishes the brawn and the utilities.

Jack's unresolved grief reminds us that when we refuse to work through a "good grief," we tend to get bogged down in denial, or to progress only to the next phase: *anger.* Turned inward, it holds the self under the gun, accusing and filling with shame. But turned outward it is keeping everybody else at bay, held hostage to a malicious spirit which has no visible root. Jack invests himself in his work, using it as a vent for the hardening and hostile unfinished business so typically the energy supply of the wounded male. But Jack knows that his unfinished business with love and fatherhood has bankrupted him emotionally. His work is drudgery. He keeps himself in debt indulging his appetite for gadgets. Nearing mid-life, his life vision has clouded over to a reality which is running near empty. At thirty-eight, life cranks on with almost nothing to show for his time on the road—without wife, without children, without a future, and without significant possesions.

HEALTHY MEN ON PARADE

The good news is that millions of men are mending today. They are those who have faced their twisted instincts to be competing, controlling tournament bucks, or systematic hoarders of money and women. They have recognized the symptoms of "self-protection" and power mongering, and have intentionally cut the nerve of those destructive instincts.

I watched Bill's tears flow on his wedding day. The assembled family and host of friends thought the uncontrolled tears signaled his deep feelings for is bride. But the three of us at the center aisle knew they were his final release of shame and guilt. Carol had, indeed, forgiven him for wasting his intimacy during high school and college years. I had said to his fiancée during an emergency session six months before, "Carol, you are a lucky woman. Not one in a hundred men would tell you the whole truth about his sexual past. Look at the risk he took in opening his entire life to you—to let you really *know* him. You could have rejected him because of his honesty with you, and he was willing to run that risk to build your relationship on complete integrity. But look at how painful the episode was when the two of you sobbed for more than an hour in dealing with his losses. This is a man who could never be unfaithful to you— there is too much pain involved in confessing the truth. But if you hold the knowledge wrapped in resentment, it is you, not Bill, who is most vulnerable to an extramarital affair—as a way of "getting back" at him.

"I was a virgin, at least technically, on our wedding day," Kyle reflected. "But I had lied to Karen. She was curious about past sexual contacts I might have had, and I took pride in my having never taken anybody to bed. But I hid the awesome battle I had with my own sexual energy. I wish I could have told her the truth about how painful it had been, and how I programmed myself into masturbation as the price paid to keep my virginity. Now, ten years into our marriage, I have finally opened up those adolescent years of frustration and shame. I wasn't vulnerable enough before, I guess."

"We are having an opportunity to see the pattern of God's grace," Rolf explained. "Jerry and I were married ten years ago. I had been a fast-lane fraternity house brat during university days, and she was devastated by her father-loss and by sexual abuse by other relatives as a child. At sixteen she gave up a baby for adoption, then followed with a couple of abortions before Jesus stabilized her as an adult. So we married knowing adoption was our only route—the last abortion cost her her uterus.

"I was never able to fault Jerry for her wild and crazy years. I had left my own tracks, and I couldn't accept God's forgiveness for me if I had held Jerry's behavior over her head. We have two adopted sons now, and every day is another miracle for us."

These composites of people I have known well, all of whom will always be important in my network of treasured friends, paint the alternatives in ways that theory rarely does. Integrity comes at an enormous price of courage and risk. But self-protection is quickly and effectively fatal. There are no cheap roads to a meaningful life. It has always been that way.

IMAGES FROM LONG AGO AND FAR AWAY

Noah preached righteousness for four hundred years, yet there is no record of his oratory. What he did was to "live integrity," I suppose. And in the low-water mark of decadence in human antiquity, his integrity fell like a mantle of protection over his family. "Just as it was in the days of Noah" (Lk. 17:26) becomes the description of conditions which will mark the end of human history. So, salute Noah as a man whose family was stabilized in the worst of times.

Joseph, favorite son in a dysfunctional polygynous family, suffered the humiliation of being sold into slavery by competitive and hateful brothers. How did Joseph survive in the crucible of that abuse? Was it his naïveté, or was it his attachment to his parents which stabilized him in Egyptian slavery? His transparent goodness won him early trust, which was undercut by a scheming Egyptian woman who wanted his body, and when spurned, punished him by falsely accusing him of attempted rape. But with his integrity and vulnerability to people intact, he became the broker of hope and truth even in prison. Released and rising in authority, Joseph spared Egypt a tragic starvation in famine, and brokered scarce food to neighboring Israeli families. Among them he found his own brothers, eventually disclosing himself to them in an episode tinctured with their terror and bathed in his tears and loud wailing at the rediscovery of family. Reunited with his father, Joseph watched his aging father as Jacob blessed Joseph's sons as a final benediction which bridged the generations—grandfather to grandsons.

Moses was marked for the ultimate abuse: infanticide. Yet his family loved him and risked protecting him. Found and reared in the Egyptian palace by the royal family, he became the national "father figure" leading the Israeli slaves out and on their way to freedom. At the low point in his political life, Moses found shelter and emotional stability in the home of the family where he would marry Ketura. And his leadership team during the Exodus consisted of his brother Aaron and his sister Miriam.

Watch another *Joseph* centuries later. He was "betrothed" to Mary, and finding her pregnant during the betrothal and knowing it was not his baby, made a tragic decision. "Because Joseph her husband was a righteous man . . . he had in mind to divorce her quietly" (Matt. 1:19).

But God confronted him and took Joseph's fear away. The heavenly message said, "Do not be afraid to take Mary home as your wife, because what is conceived in her is from the Holy Spirit. She will give birth to a son, and you are to give him the name Jesus, because he will save his people from their sins" (Matt. 1:20).

So Joseph not only provided the name Jesus, but furnished the legal registry for his permanent genealogy. You can read it in Matthew's first chapter. But equally important, Joseph gave Jesus the care and nurture that only a father can give a boy, so that Jesus grew up in healthy maturity: in wisdom, in physique, and in healthy relationships with God and others.

Then, finally, at the apex of his teaching ministry, Jesus returned the compliment to Joseph. As he was teaching the disciples to pray, Jesus gave God a new name.

The sovereign *Elohim, Yahweh-Jehovah, El Shaddai,* and *Adoni* names became, on Jesus' lips, "Our Father"! On another occasion Jesus even used "Daddy, Father,"— "Abba," in which you can almost hear the near universal "Papa." And where do you think Jesus learned the meaning of those syllables?

JOIN THE "REAL MEN" CLUB!

A new fraternity is forming all over the world. Already you can begin to identify some of the members. They are men who are being transformed from one degree of powerful gentleness to another, and this comes directly from God's grace. They are assertive, but unconditionally controlled by respect for the value of people. They are tough-minded, but full of tenderness in their relationships.

The Old Testament canon closes with a description of the forming of a new breed of man. There is a single "marker," a solitary characteristic of these rehabilitated men. You can spot one in an instant. The test criterion is named here in the final words of the book of Malachi: "See, I will send you the prophet Elijah before that great and dreadful day of the Lord comes. He will turn the hearts of the fathers to their children, and the hearts of the children to their fathers" (Mal. 4:5-6). So the call is clear: The real "survivalists" will be the tough but tender fathers who are devoted to the nurture and care of children, and their transformation will be in response to the call of Elijah. "When Elijah comes" represents the undying hope that justice and truth will one day control the world.

Those of us who link the Old Testament with the New, trace the connection through Elijah. Because when he finally comes Elijah turns out to be John the Baptist— that tough and gentle final prophet. Zechariah receives the clear prophetic word from an angel: "He will be a joy and delight to you, and many will rejoice because of his birth, for he will be great in the sight of the Lord. He is never to take wine or other fermented drink, and he will be filled with the Holy Spirit even from birth. Many of the people of Israel will he bring back to the Lord their God. And he will go on before the Lord, in the spirit and power of Elijah, to turn the hearts of the fathers to their children and the disobedient to the wisdom of the righteous—to make ready a people prepared for the Lord—(Lk. 1:14-17).

This outdoorsman, complete with a stress camper's diet and hooked deep into the masculine spirit, sanctified men's hearts, turning them into effective and affectionate fathers, shutting down their "idols" of work, consumption, and obscenity by sanctifying their male energy into the service of what is good, true, holy, and constructive.

Then, to complete the profile of membership in the "Real Men Club," Jesus comments both on John the Baptist and on the roles of toughness, aggressiveness, even "violence" required of healthy males:

Jesus began to speak to the people about John: "What was the spectacle that drew you to the wilderness? A reed-bed swept by the wind? [Denoting ambivalence, wishy-washiness.] No? Then what did you go out to see? A man dressed in silks and satins? [Denoting the soft, effeminate career and *Peter Pan* types.] Surely you must look in palaces for that. But why did you go out? To see a prophet? [Denoting one who predicts the future.] Yes, indeed, and far more than a prophet. He is the man of whom Scripture says, 'Here is my herald, whom I send on ahead of you, and he will prepare your way before you.' I tell you this: Never has there appeared on earth a mother's son greater than John the Baptist, and yet the least in the kingdom of Heaven is greater than he.

Ever since the coming of John the Baptist, the

kingdom of Heaven has been subjected to violence and violent men are seizing it." [Literally, taking it by violence.] For all the prophets and the Law foretold things to come until John appeared, and John is the destined Elijah, if you will but accept it. If you have ears, then hear" (Matt. 11:7-15, NEB).

Luke captures the "violence" sense a little differently: "The Law and the Prophets were proclaimed until John. Since that time, the good news of the kingdom of God is being preached, and everyone is forcing his way into it" (Luke 16:16, my translation).

The imagery is pretty troublesome to our "silk and satin" view of feminized religion. The text uses John the Baptist—the "Elijah" messenger, as the focal point of violence: His announcing Jesus produced a violent response among those who rejected the call to integrity, obedience, repentance, and turning from wicked, deceitful, and indulgent living. Then, the silk and satin crowd was left standing in the dust as the "violent" sinners of all sorts took Jesus seriously and stormed into repentance and repudiation of their past wickedness. These storm troops were the unwashed rabble who grabbed on to Jesus' words and took him seriously.

It is clear why many men have little to do with "silk and satin" churches today. They have to park their masculinity at the door, and nothing "violent" has been announced or grasped in many congregations for generations. And when a man has a clear built-in altimeter which gives him a reading on issues of truth and justice, you can understand why he cannot tolerate a wishy-washy religious environment. Is there no truth to stick by? Is any road as good as another to find your way to heaven? To hell? If so, then most men will say, "Forget it!" and they'll go fishing.

But give a man permission to tap into his considerable sense of justice, his grasp of what is true, and his need for making a muscular and visceral response, and watch out. The real men are ready for action.

NO MEMBERSHIP CARD NEEDED
Welcome to the club of men under reconstruction—those who are being made whole, complete, and well. Accept the legitimacy of your male energy. Embrace the destiny of being a responsible manager of your sexual energy, letting it fuel your intimacy, your parenting, your productivity, your "expansiveness," and your creativity. Let integrity, courage, and gentleness be your middle names. You will not only have made peace with your past, but the future belongs to you, and with your surging energy, you will take it forcefully and with dignity.

ELEVEN

◇

STRATEGIES FOR SUPPORT NETWORKS

Kevin stumbled by accident into one of my formation groups. It was nearly fifteen years ago, now. For three years I had cooperated as a lunch group formed around me in the cafeteria. Randy had initiated the whole thing in the fall of his second year. He approached me saying, "I'm cranking out of here right on schedule, which means I won't have any more courses with you, but would you be willing to spend an hour a week with me? I still haven't found out everything I want to know about you."

He frightened me with those invasive words, so I bought time and diluted the threat of a one-on-one situation responding, "See if you can find a couple of other guys, then let's meet over a brown-bag lunch or in the dining commons. I would enjoy that."

The Tuesday lunch group turned into a daily session. It was largely unstructured, but I evoked the members' stories in several layers across each year. When Randy graduated, so did most of his friends. Only Dan was left, and he had inquired whether we would continue. We decided to "go fishing" by taking a large round table in the dining commons to plan a list of guys we might invite.

Before we got a single name on paper, Kevin walked up, brown bag in hand asking, "Can I eat with you guys?" I had met Kevin on our curriculum committee that had clocked endless hours the previous year. Dan knew him as a classroom acquaintance. He joined us, but we shut down our planning for the new group. We enjoyed our time with Kevin, whose bright and incisive mind quickly became our catalyst on that Tuesday.

Wednesday, Dan and I were seated at the same table, yellow pad out to begin our work, when in came Kevin again!

"Shall we tell him what we're doing?" I probed Dan.

"Why not?" he responded.

So Kevin was our first recruit, and before Thursday, the other contacts were made to fill the table. That year, it expanded and included a couple of students' wives. Eating together Tuesday through Friday each week, we soon clocked enough hours to really know each other.

The school year went quickly. In May when Kevin was graduating, our phone rang. "Who is Robbie sitting with at Baccalaureate and Commencement?" Kevin probed.

"No one in particular. Why do you ask?"

"Well, Darlene will be by herself, and most people have family here. I didn't want her to feel all alone. Could she sit with Robbie?"

"Not only that, but you and Darlene are our dinner guests. Let's make a day of it. We always eat in the student center on Commencement day."

We weren't so slow to pick up the clues after that. After Kevin became a Christian in high school, his father had emotionally disowned him. His dad also resented Kevin's leading his younger brothers to faith. His father had effectively shut down all family contact and, though wealthy, had made certain that no support went to Kevin during college or seminary training.

As they were loading their U-Haul to leave Wilmore, Robbie and I invited them to spend their last night with us. We saw them off the next morning—a ritual we celebrate as we populate the planet with our prized friends. But we were not prepared for the courtesy note that came within a week from Darlene to Robbie. She added, "P.S. Say thanks to Don for inviting Kevin into his group this year. Kevin has been more kind to me ever since he started meeting with Don and the group."

MEN AS LONERS

I experience the cosmic loneliness that is common to human males. Recognizing this, I long ago made choices to intentionally establish contact with others. Here are some of the disciplines I practice to systematically break out of my isolation:

Get out of the house. Men who punch time clocks have their world carved up into segments that order their movement. Two of my careers have been largely self-employed experiences. Because of this, I find that I need to get up, get out, and get going into some productive activity before daylight. Fortunately for our marriage, Robbie thrives on the same pattern. Both of us have small spans of time in our history when we did not follow the "get up and get out" pattern, and both of us drifted into mild depressions. Getting out of the house, I find, puts me in the world of other people, and makes me available to others. Most of my writing is done during the early hours between six and nine in the morning. I find myself eagerly suggesting to seminary men who are nonproductive, depressed, lethargic, or losing their focus: "If you're married, get out of the house at the same moment your wife leaves, or at least an hour before your first class. Take charge of your early morning."

Speak first, even if you forget the name. I am profoundly introverted. But about twenty years ago, I made an important change. When encountering another person in the hallway or grocery store, I always speak first. And, since I am by Creation preference introverted, I lose names quickly unless I say the name at least three times when I first meet the person. The rhetoric sometimes gets ridiculous as I attempt that feat. So, I do two conscious and intentional things. I address the eyes of the person, and I allow my affective energy to greet the person warmly. If the name is not instantly on my tongue, I tell the truth: "I've lost your name." People typically give their names easily if you sustain direct eye contact with them.

I do those intentional things, because they are exactly what I wish people would do with me, if they value me. I have given myself permission to reach out and touch someone with my eyes and my voice, and I do it often. It would be easier for me to slip into the supermarket, study the shelves, and sneak through the checkout line engaging virtually no eyes. My introversion thrives on that approach. But I would be indulging in what is not good for humans—being alone. Indeed, I have so many projects going most of the time that I can entirely envelop myself in my own many agendas, walking like a masked man around campus. My solution is to consciously and intentionally present myself to other people.

Make time for informal social contact. Married or not, it is important to generate a network of friends. In the opening chapter of my *Bonding: Relationships in the Image of God,* I report on a famous psychiatrist's findings that each of us needs a minimum of twenty people in our network. I refer to it as the "hand-held trampoline" of significant people who hang on while we celebrate and while we grieve. It takes time to build relationships—time you could have been making money, or pursuing a private hobby.

Robbie and I vacation three times each year with the same five to seven couples. Two couple friendships are potentially troublesome with the mixed messages that may evolve, so we have found great comfort in our multiple-couple friendships. We have been doing our intentional vacationing together now for nearly twenty years; we are growing old together. But this sustained vacationing has brought our hearts and lives together so that we are healthier and stronger than if we did not have each other.

Just off campus, we have been meeting each month now for fifteen years with five faculty couples. When death struck we hung on even tighter to the survivor, and in spite of her international professional circuit, we book group events to match her Kentucky stops.

Beyond this, we try to schedule a monthly show and tell session, usually over dessert or dinner, with our adult children. This serves to keep us abreast of the news breaking in our fully-packed lives. Further, Robbie manages to run a "Grandchildren Hotel" an average of twice a month as we take one of the sets of our three grandchildren to keep current with the best link to the future that God has given us.

I list these as my own disclosure of social agendas. We all have different avenues and opportunities for informal fellowship. Robbie and I have shaken down our priorities, and the preceding are our nonnegotiable minimum contacts. We celebrate the fact that God's principle is right, it is very good that humans be together.

Be systematic about same-sex accountability and support. Males in virtually every warm-blooded species are playful and "social" in infancy and pre-adult development. But the patterns of isolation sweep across the species when they arrive at sexual maturity. The competitive tournament male isolates in order to win and sometimes to protect his "harem" of females. This reproductive "business" dominates his life, and his social circle of male peers is eliminated. What is worse, competitive males so dominate their females and so isolate themselves from infant care and female issues, that they are

Unfinished Business

largely rejected from female social contact. The "lonely stag," the isolated stallion, and the dangerous and violent bull are images that are painful to contemplate.

Human males tend to move into isolation and competition when they enter adulthood. Yet the years from 13 to 25 may see them moving in an "extended play" phase in our popular culture. However, this apparent extention of childhood innocence tends to be hollow, as Erik Erikson cautioned us it would be. If genuine "intimacy" is not established with a woman, the male, however visibly active he may be, moves into emotional and developmental "isolation."

A man is on the road to health and wholeness when he can face his own need for sexual intimacy by establishing his exclusive lifelong loving nest with a woman and their children, and at the same time stabilizing his additional social needs by maintaining a significant core group of trusted and equally vulnerable male friends. The man who, for any reason, does not establish the intimate nest with the "opposite" female dimension of his reality, can, as a viable alternative, make an integrity commitment to intentional sexual celibacy combined with maintenance of two trusted and vulnerable support clusters—one male and one female.

In this chapter, I will be offering the male network agendas I have found useful in hosting support groups and in initiating accountability within groups who continue without my participation.

FORMING AND SHAPING A GROUP

"I have some things I want to work on over the next several weeks. And, frankly, I find that everytime I'm around you I leave realizing that you've taught me something—even when you don't say much. What hour of the week might work best for getting together? I'd like to pull in a couple of other guys too. What would you think of that?"

How would you respond to such a phone call? Look at

181

Strategies for Support Networks

~~S·pp~~ ~~Gr~~~~oups~~

what the proposal suggests:
1. A one-hour weekly meeting.
2. Intentional agenda—"some things."
3. A group of up to four men.
4. Voluntary participation.
5. Sustained time—"the next several weeks."

Many men are dying on the vine and would leap at the opportunity for an intentional support group. Think of what they face: career decisions, marital questions, parenting problems, coping with the seductions of culture, job frustration, and deeper personal integrity issues.

Men meet in bars, tell stories, make confessions, laugh and cry, bump, slap, and hug each other—all gestures denoting deep needs to establish relationships with others. Men hunt, fish, play golf, watch television sports, and go to service club luncheons and prayer breakfasts together. But what characterizes most of these contacts is their superficiality. It has been my experience that "intentional agenda" is the missing ingredient in most of these group experiences.

But for every man who goes to the Rotary, Silver Bullet, or prayer breakfast, there are likely ten more who move like zombies through their daily and weekend routine. Many resort to the weekend anesthesia of *Michelob*, and only deepen their isolation from wife and children. If any group of men needs intentional agenda accountability with peers, it is these men who drop more deeply into the isolated and lonely male syndrome. Often these men reduce themselves, almost systematically, to a robotic wasteland of punching time clocks, performing jobs, picking up checks, then checking out of the human race until Monday morning.

Do you find yourself in such a rut? If so, let me challenge you to respond to the following questions:
1. Who might share my need for accountability and support?
2. What immediate questions would I be willing to

risk airing with some peers?

3. What time and plan might work?

Are you serious about resolving the unfinished business in your life? Then after answering these questions, get ready to make your first phone call.

WATCHING THE SUPPORT NETWORK DEVELOP

Facilitator. Anybody can start a group and maintain it, identify the agenda, and open and close meetings. Most groups quickly emerge with a system of their own. Week-by-week responsibility might float, with only light maintenance by the founder or other emerging coordinator.

One group member may emerge as a genius at organizing and facilitating. Normally the group would want that member, not necessarily the inviting founder, to utilize his gift of leadership. Dogmatic, high control, Type-A personalities rarely tend to accept an invitation to lead unless they imagine the group to be a vehicle for some personal goal of their own. The leader must communicate that the group needs to be seen as time out from work, competition, and achievement. Group time is a gift each one presents to the others. For some men it will be difficult to give themselves permission to enjoy meeting with peers for even an hour a week.

Fidelity listening. I have found that the strength of any group of men is directly related to a couple of essentials. Members need to listen carefully enough to check out whether understanding is happening in their conversations. This means that as important material is on the table, it is all right to interrupt to clarify what someone is saying. I sometimes interrupt someone who seems to be responding or making a speech to ask the previous speaker whether we have abandoned his question or agenda.

The time factor. Significant groups that perform good work in problem-solving, support, and question-asking are successful because of the amount of time spent together in regular participation. The rule of thumb is this: Effective support requires building a foundation whose layers consist of as many hours by the clock as the number of men who are in the group. So, when someone misses two sessions, a group of four or five is effectively held up and must start over to accumulate the basic time investment. When I suggest agenda models later in this chapter, you will notice that history-giving starters are the best investment during the foundational phase of group support.

Regular participation. Nobody can make every meeting. But fidelity of presence should be aimed for. This means that everybody will be, as the old idiom has it, "present, or accounted for." Delinquency without accountability for absence is likely a signal that the group is not a priority. Perhaps it did not turn out to serve the purposes which the member had originally hoped for. "Can you come back one more time," I've sometimes said, "and simply check out with the guys so we don't simply feel like we've dropped you or you've dropped us? We are all adults, and whenever someone needs to leave we can handle that." Such closure is important if everyone is to maintain a sense of integrity, and such an invitation signals the deep commitment of the group to being adult, responsible, and able to "set free" anyone who needs to give priority to something else.

CHOOSING YOUR AGENDAS
Begin, of course, with the presenting task, problem, or decision on which you need to get feedback. If you convene people you already know, you can get right to business. The best agendas are always those rising out of the life needs of the participants.

I normally have a light agenda through which my groups are working at any given time, but after we have our foundational hours invested, I consistently inquire, "Does anybody have something you need to work on today, before we take up the ongoing agenda?" This puts people ahead of agendas, and the energy in a well-established group marvelously and magnetically attaches to the person and the issue.

We might as well admit it. Most of us do not know other people and are not known well by others outside of our immediate families. All too often even they do not really know who we are. For that reason, I use a number of nonthreatening agendas to encourage others to be vulnerable. Most of these are history-giving invitations. Most of us would hesitate to take up the time of our busy friends to talk about ourselves in this way. But when the plan calls for us to hear the same sort of story from all participants, we tend to be ready to lay out our stories.

HISTORY GIVING

To prompt history giving I have an absolutely nonthreatening first round I use with backpacking trail families and men's support groups alike. It is one of those licenses we all enjoy having issued to us. The task is to describe the thing you did as a kid (ambiguous enough to envelop everything from birth to leaving home) that your parents still laugh about.

The facilitator who announces the task, of course, always begins with his own story. The invitation is a simple appeal, "Let us laugh with you too."

Over the longer haul, nothing has served our groups better than working through the "age twenty transition" agendas from Daniel J. Levinson's findings in *The Seasons of a Man's Life*. There are agenda items for the age thirty, forty, and fifty transitions as well, but adult men have all been into or through the "age twenty transition," so we have stuck with it as our history-giving foundational agenda.

Levinson, looking for a way to locate and describe "mid-life crisis" found that men do, indeed, have one. But he found that his forty-one men had a crisis every ten years, not simply a mid-life one! All men, evidently, have to wrestle sometime between seventeen and twenty-three with the same issues. We simply tell stories which illustrate how we were dealing with each of the items. It works best, we have found, to listen to everybody on one layer before moving to the second issue. Here are the four layers of the age twenty agenda his men had to work through:

1. How did you break away and establish yourself as a person independent of your family?

2. Who was your mentor, a significant model who knew you were fixing your sights on that model, during the 17-23 years?

3. What was your life vision? What did you imagine yourself doing and being as an adult?

4. How did you attempt to establish intimacy with a woman between your 17th and 23rd years?

Men must be prompted to respond to these questions and most agenda items with "stories." The stories need to be descriptive: populated with people who have names, quoting actual words spoken, and recreating action visibly. Unfortunately, the left-brain analytical male resists such detailed sharing, thinking only in abstract or summary terms. The storytelling form is crucial, because it forces men to open up.

THE PAINFUL PROBES

Below, you will find a response sheet which I have asked my men's groups to complete. Answered anonymously, they are able to "rank order" the importance of items in their hidden agendas. Also, they are able to rank items which did not appear on the list. I tabulate the unsigned sheets, then return the sheets for each man to retrieve and refer to while we are sharing. We then work with our personal lists each week, sharing personal memories and stories about our pasts. During these times we discover we are a fellowship of like-sufferers, with common concerns. Unfortunately, much of the pain we carry is magnified by our feelings that nobody else has ever been through what we're experiencing.

OUR HIDDEN AGENDAS

Instructions: Rank order the five things which bother or worry you the most out of your past or present experiences. No one else will see your sheet. Fold it and carry it in your wallet. We will simply use the lists as springboards for telling our own stories.

1 Feelings of emotional abandonment or abuse by my mother.

2 Feelings of emotional abandonment or abuse by my father.

3 Preschool sexual exploration—peers equally inexperienced.

4 Preschool sexual abuse/incest—used sexually by an older person.

5 Brother or sister rivalry—unresolved competition.

6 Adolescent sexual exploration—peers equally inexperienced.

7 Adolescent sexual abuse—seduced by a more experienced person.

8 Genital contact before marriage, partner(s) other than spouse.

9 Genital contact with spouse before marriage.

10 Feelings of confusion about my career/vocation/calling.

11 Feeling inadequate/unworthy/unreliable for my vocation.

12 Feelings of incompetence and "faking it" much of the time.

13 Unable to ever please my father/mother.

14 Inability to express my feelings.

15 Uncertain whether I am worth loving and respecting.

16 Worry that I may be over-sexed, that I masturbated too early, too late, too long, too much, even now.

17 Worry that I may be sexually addicted, consistent-

ly, and compulsively, and destructively attracted toward using other people.
18 Worry that I am vulnerable to sexual inversion.
19 Occasional use, or silent rehearsal of obscene/
vulgar language.
20 Feelings that I am vulnerable or that I am
dangerous.
21 Other worries:

THE MACHO DIAGNOSIS

The "Marlboro man" is at once the idol of our culture
and a symbol of human civilization since the edge of
Eden. In chapters 7 and 8, I unravelled the amazing story
of the origin of the "macho scar" and some effective
ways to soften and heal its desensitized toughness.

Following is another response sheet I have used. It is
an agenda for men who want to examine their macho
roots as they begin to tell the truth, do their grieving,
and become compassionate and whole men again.

IDENTIFYING THE ROOTS OF THE MACHO FACADE

Instructions: Use these lists of possible sources of
pain or stress to "revisit" your childhood, adolescence, and past adult years. For each of those age-lev-
el categories, pause and try to remember and to feel
again what you felt then. Recall how you managed to
survive, what decisions you made, and what your
reasons were for making the choices you did.

Present Patterns
Here are typical "macho" symptoms you may be
displaying:
1 Self-justifying anger—dumping blame on other
people when things go wrong or dumping the shame
on them for your own feelings of failure.
2 No-risk relationships, held at arm's length.

3 "Bristling" competitive, distancing from male peers.

4 Instrumental (flirtatious/sexual) overtures with females.

Search: Look in these places and tell your story in each season:

Early childhood:

1 Withdrawal of parental affection, attention, or comfort at a time when you felt vulnerable, sick, helpless, or needy.

2 Parental, sibling, or significant other "abuse."

3 Abandonment by parent, or significant other.

Adolescence:

1 Peer or parental betrayal or abuse.

2 Abandonment by a first or an early love.

3 Substituting artificial pleasures/highs for investment in relationships with risk possibilities.

4 Substituting success for vulnerability and investment in relationships.

Adulthood:

1 Abandonment or abuse by spouse or child, perhaps your wife's forsaking you during the first pregnancy, or her persistent giving of first priority to the children.

2 Feelings of self-pity at such abandonment.

3 Betrayal of or infidelity with a significant person.

4 Substituting work, success, money, or instrumental pleasures for vulnerability and investment in relationships.

Strategies for dissolving the macho facade: Revisit the scene of the early injury, and grieve the loss:

1 Give yourself permission to hurt and cry, even now, for pain and loss which you have stored in denial.

2 Reconstruct the environment of withdrawn affection, or the painful episode of injury, abuse, or abandonment.

3 Write the "story" in letter form as if you were speaking to the offender and fixing blame.

4 Name your losses (include these in the letters) and describe your feelings then: helplessness, anger, "raped," violated, hurt, devastated, or worthless.

5 Work through each earlier episode you identified with pain or loss, but this time revisit the painful experience *with your present integrity and strength* dominating the scene. Tell the hurt or failing person you were that you will solve the problem now, that you are wiser and better equipped to deal with the episode. Sometimes you need to forgive your person of the past for his bad choices. If Jesus has forgiven you, for example, be sure you go back and assure the little boy that he is forgiven and thank him for "being there" and for managing to survive with so many things going wrong. As you forgive him, let him be your hero too.

BREAKING SEXUAL ADDICTION

Millions of secretly compulsive men must have shuddered when a prominent television evangelist was shown on network television. He had been photographed in a motel parking lot with a prostitute. Now, he was making his public confession: "Why? Why? Why! I have asked myself that question a thousand times!"

In this book I have set down the amazing facts about male sexuality and development which set the young man up to be profoundly vulnerable to compulsive sexual activity.

1. Male sexuality is hormonally charged, and
2. his fertility is "locked in" to the highest pleasure.
3. His sexual anatomy is the basic affirmation of his

Unfinished Business

male identity, but

4. his sexuality is shrouded in privacy and secrecy

5. as preparation for "presentation" to his exclusive lifelong woman—his wife.

6. Since male sex is highly charged and profoundly personal and private,

7. most males do not develop language and basic knowledge which is constructive, rich, and ennobling to this best gift of their personhood.

8. So the typical male lives in embarrassed "denial" of his need for tenderness and meaning, and indulges in secret, embarrassing, but titillating sexual experiences which leave his deepest needs frustrated and wrapped in further humiliation and shame.

Any man who examines how his sexual energy has been expressed is looking at high-voltage resources that could have been diverted into compulsive, self-gratifying behaviors. In an environment of accountability, most men can come to terms with their imagination and sexual behavior and find that it loses its compulsive, driven characteristics. Compulsive behavior follows a pattern that is secretly launched by a powerful, often *trance-like desire*. If the behavior is not intercepted during the desire phase, it moves into an almost hypnotically carried out *ritual* which has been developed because it delivers the payoff *episode* (food, sex, alcohol, drugs, power, exhilaration). The episode is the climax event, which is followed by feelings of shame—humiliation, depression, and failure. Most people with one compulsive addiction have two or three, so when they are depressed over one failure, they often "kick in" another trancelike preoccupation and are off on a second Ferris wheel of "trance-ritual-episode-shame," in a circus of destroying their self-respect.

Many of us began our compulsive behaviors in innocence, often under peer influence that left us running on empty from the first episode. Sexual addiction tends to arise out of a catalytic environment or event. The catalytic environment most often turns out to have been during our childhood. Any situation in which self-esteem is at major risk, in which significant adults do not maintain an orderly, predictable, and safe environment, or where marital stress, alcoholism, family separation, divorce, or abuse is present is an atmosphere in which compulsive behavior can be spawned.

However, the catalytic event is more often some happening during adolescence or adulthood. It often consists of an intense vulnerability or unpredictable collapse of integrity caused by an untimely assault,

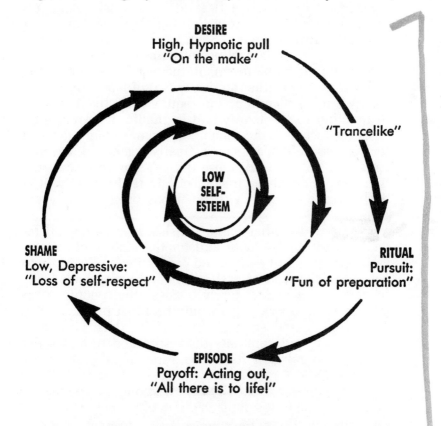

seduction, or "opportunity" for relief through wild experimentation. The devastation to self-esteem can be so traumatic that a cycle of addiction seems to instantly be set in motion. Shame is the motor which drives the behavior, producing more humiliation in an increasing crescendo, cycle after cycle.

It is shame, not guilt, which burrows a black hole in the personality as compulsive behavior digs a deeper and deeper pit of negative self-judgments. Shame builds more privacy and more careful rituals, until in final desperation it may drive the person either toward self-destruction by taking a flagrant public risk, making a violent attempt to destroy the marriage and family, or even committing suicide. Shame consists of a cluster of narcissistic wounds: feelings of humiliation, fear of discovery, public embarrassment, inadequacy, and of being a sham. Shame further erodes self-confidence, makes integrity a mere phantom, and requires effective cover-up to function in the family and in public. It provides no basis for recovery and rehabilitation, or redemption and forgiveness. When shame is finally tracked down and caught, it refuses to disclose the full pattern of destructive behavior and the history of failure. Inevitably, it is willing only to deal with what has been publicly exposed.

Guilt, on the other hand, consists of owning full responsibility for behavior and for the history of failure. Guilt motors a full and a good confession and is eager to get the whole load of past failure and private misdeeds named and owned. It rarely blames other people, even though an objective judge would find that responsibility should be shared among others. Guilt, thus, is able to make a full and complete disclosure and provides the essential foundation for redemption, restitution, rehabilitation, and forgiveness.

When a man can identify his own compulsive tendencies and name them among a group of peers in a support environment, the addiction cycle can be broken. Patrick

Carnes has identified a "Twelve Step" program for supporting people who are recovering from sexual addiction. It is outlined in his book, *Out of the Shadows: Understanding Sexual Addiction.*

Sexaholics Anonymous has developed a self-help group process available in most major cities. It too follows the "Twelve Step" pattern first developed by Alcoholics Anonymous. But here are my own adaptations of the Twelve Steps, which I call Twelve Steps Plus:[1]

TWELVE STEPS PLUS

1. We admitted that we were powerless over our compulsive behavior—that our lives had become unmanageable, and we voluntarily reached out to trusted people for help.

2. We came to see that God mediates His grace through trusted people who listen unconditionally, offer forgiveness, demand accountability, and walk with us in the redeeming community of Jesus.

3. Thus forgiven, accountable, and affirmed, we accepted God's sanctifying grace with its day-by-day cleansing of our thoughts, words, relationships, and behaviors.

4. We wrote a searching and fearless moral inventory of our past behavior and addiction, both reducing the past to an objective record to free our subjective consciences, and providing an agenda for restitution and sacrificial reconciliation.

5. We appealed for divine forgiveness by confessing responsibility for our behavior to God and by naming the exact nature of our wrongs to a spiritual director with whom we shared our inventory of past failure and addiction in a support group.

6. We surrendered our attachment to those addictive behaviors and asked God to heal all of these present defects of character, as well as to heal their roots and traces throughout our past lives.

7. We humbly asked God to remove our shortcomings

and our tendencies to drift into isolation and into compulsive behavior.

8. We made a list of all persons we had harmed and became willing to make amends to them all.

9. We made direct restitution to all people we had wronged wherever possible, except when to do so would have injured them or other people.

10. We continue to take personal inventory and when we are wrong promptly admit it and acknowledge that we are continually recovering from our past deformities.

11. We are seeking through prayer and meditation to improve our conscious contact with God, seeking for knowledge to know His will for us and for the power to carry that out.

12. Having had a profound moral and spiritual renewal as a result of these steps, we are trying to carry this message of hope and healing to others and to practice these principles in all of our activities.

In my *Re-bonding: Preventing and Restoring Damaged Relationships*, I explore additional steps for healing from broken relationships, especially where adultery and promiscuity have been involved. The support group pattern needs to be invested over a minimum of one year of faithful weekly sessions, to predict significant stabilization and the ability to cope without group accountability. But every man needs lifelong significant support in an intentional network simply to remain a healthy and growing person.

This chapter of guidelines and resources for getting men into intentional support networks ends the book. The whole journey here has been an invitation to abandon self-protection with the painful isolation that inevitably follows. But these outlines and agendas are only tentative suggestions. You will generate more appropriate and urgent conversation as you act on your courage to get honest with other men.

Unfinished Business is my open confession for all of us who are finding that the integrity journey's finish line remains always ahead of us. We never "have it made." But like the Apostle Paul, we find exhilaration in the race and we press on toward the finish line of the high calling of God in Christ Jesus. And day by day we are increasingly sure that the path of the just is like the rising sun, which shines more and more brightly as it reaches the perfect zenith of the day.

Notes

Chapter One

1. See the notes for Genesis 5 in a NIV Bible. Note the footnote inside the closing quototation mark around "man." It is anybody's guess why the translators did not provide the footnote in Genesis 1, with the first appearance of "man." In the thirteenth century someone "pointed" certain appearances of 'A-dam" suggesting that they would be distinguished between generic "man" and the male "Adam." But older manuscripts have no such separating clues. So we simply would help ourselves to always read Adam or "man" as "the Adamses." At least then we are ready for all of the plural charges "Let them have dominion," for example.

2. Frank H. Netter, *The Ciba Collection of Medical Illustrations*, Vol. 2, "A Compilation of Paintings on the Normal and Pathologic Anatomy of the Reproductive System" (New York: Ciba Pharmaceutical Company, 1965). See Section I, Plate 1, "Homologues of Internal Genita-

Unfinished Business

lia," and Section I, Plate 2, "Homologues of External Genitalia," pp. 2 and 3, to trace the male-female developmental differentiation in the stages reported in this chapter. For an extended description of these fetal development features see also my *Bonding: Relationships in the Image of God*, (Dallas: Word, Inc., 1985), especially chapter 5, "Conception: Differentiating the Adam," pp. 87–107. You can follow the sexual differentiation process by watching the PBS series, *The Body Human: The Sexes*, or you can read about it in M. J. Sherfey, *The Nature and Evolution of Female Sexuality*, (New York: Vintage, revised, 1972). If you want to track down a popularized version, including the brain transformation which is described later in this chapter, see Pamela Weintraub, "The Brain: His and Hers," in *Discover*, April 1981, pp. 15ff.

3. The sexual orientation issue in relation to defective male fetal development is reported in Robert W. Goy and Bruce S. McEwen, *Sexual Differentiation in the Brain*, (Cambridge: MIT Press, 1980), especially in the subsection, "Is There an Endocrine Basis for Homosexuality Among Human Males?" pp. 64ff. The medical judgments are that prevention and rehabilitation, along with positive "masculinity support" in the environment are the obligations of the family and the medical community. Verifying the power of positive male brain development to compensate for overwhelming negative environmental damage is the astonishing report on the Dominican third-world "laboratory" in which thirty-eight mutant defect males were discovered who began life with complete female external genitalia. The group, spanning four generations and twenty-three interrelated families, was studied beginning in 1972. By a fluke in timing (the 5α-Reductase Factor), although their ovaries were modified internally and were functioning as testicles and the brain was fully masculinized, the testicles remained inside the body. These "girls" were actually thinking like

boys, even though the penis development and the dropping of the testicles did not occur until the onset of pubescence. So in a culture in which young boys remained naked until pubescence and young girls wore panties and the only bathing place was the open river, these "boy" were programmed to have sexual orientation appropriate to their rearing and public "identity." Yet of the twenty-five surviving, of which nineteen have been studied in detail, seventeen are living as normal males in common-law marriages. One is a rural bachelor living as a male. One co-habits with a woman as a male, but presents himself publicly as a woman. So the "environment" versus "physiological" basis for sexual orientation has given us new concerns about physiology. The environment of the Dominican Republic males, however, was powerfully clear on sexual differentiation and sex-appropriate behavior. The seventeen males who married did so at an average of one year later than their non-defective male peers. In a culture which gives mixed signals or even "mocks" its young boys' interest in girls, and subjects its adolescents to confusing, ambiguous, and politically attractive forms of rebellion to assert independence of family and traditional cultural values, an actual magnet might be made of sexual inversion. You can read about the Dominican discovery in the chief researcher's own words in Julianne Imperato-McGinley, "Androgens and the Evolution of Male-Gender Identity Among Male Pseudohermaphrodites with 5a-Reductase Deficiency" in *The New England Journal of Medicine*, May 31, 1979, pp. 1233ff.

4. See Diane McGuinness, "How Schools Discriminate Against Boys," in *Human Nature*, February, 1979, pp. 82–88.

5. J. D. Unwin, *Sex and Culture*, 3 Vols., summarized in *Sexual Regulations and Human Behavior* (London: Williams & Northgate, 1933), and in an address to the Medi-

cal Section of the British Psychological Society in 1935, *Sexual Regulations and Cultural Behaviour* (London: Oxford University Press, 1935).

Chapter Two

1. Thomas Parish and J. Dostal, "Relationships Between Evaluations of Self and Parents by Children from Intact and Divorced Families," in *The Journal of Psychology*, 1980, Vol. 104, pp. 35–38. See also Parish's many other research reports, including, "Evaluations of Self and Parent Figures by Children from Intact, Divorced and Reconstituted Families," *Journal of Youth and Adolescence*, 1980, Vol. 19, pages 347–51, and "The Impact of Divorce and Subsequent Father Absence on Children's and Adolescents' Self-Concepts" with James C. Taylor, *Journal of Youth and Adolescence*, Vol. 8, 1979, pp. 427–32.

2. George Gilder, *Men and Marriage*, revised and expanded from *Sexual Suicides* (Gretna, La.: Pelican, 1986), p. 6.

3. Arthur Miller, *Death of a Salesman* (New York: The Viking Press, 1950), from pages 118–21.

4. Dan Kiley, *The Peter Pan Syndrome* (New York: Dodd & Mead, 1983).

5. Kenneth Druck, *The Secrets Men Keep: Breaking the Silence Barrier* (Garden City, N.Y.: Doubleday and Co., 1985).

Chapter Three

1. See Rebecca Cann, et al, "Mitochondrial DNA and Human Evolution." *Nature*, Vol. 325, Jan. 1, 1987, pp. 31ff., as well as "Out of the Garden of Eden," p. 13, same

issue. Consider, too, *Time*, Jan. 26, 1987, "Everyone's Genealogical Mother," p. 66, and the PBS video special, "Children of Eve," Jan. 27, 1987.

2. For Myers-Briggs basic interpretation see Isabel Briggs Myers, *Introduction to Type*, and *Gifts Differing* (Palo Alto: Consulting Psychologists Press, 1980, both publications). See David Keirsey and Marilyn Bates, *Please Understand Me* (Del Mar: Prometheus Nemesis, 1978), p. 20, for the male/female divergence on the "Thinking-Feeling" spectrum.

3. Sheldon and Eleanor Glueck, *Unravelling Juvenile Delinquency* (Cambridge: Harvard University Press, 1950). For the data on the New York City Youth Board experiment, see Maude M. Craig and Selma J. Glick, *A Manual of Procedures for Application of the Glueck Prediction Table* (New York: Youth Board Research Institute of New York, 1965).

4. Herman Hesse, *Narcissus and Goldmund*, Tr. by Ursule Molinaro (New York: Farrar, Straus and Giroux, 1968).

Chapter Four

1. Paul Tournier, *Secrets* (Richmond: John Knox Press, 1965).

2. For further information see chapter 1, note #2.

Chapter Five

1. C.S. Lewis, "As the Ruin Falls," in *Poems* (New York: Harcourt Brace Jovanovich, Inc., 1964), pp. 109–10.

2. Paul Pearsall, *Super-Marital Sex: Loving for Life* (New York: Ballantine, 1987), p. 71.

Unfinished Business

3. See my chapters, "Pair Bonding: What God Joins Together," and "What Has Gone Wrong with the Bonding?' in my *Bonding: Relationships in the Image of God* (Dallas: Word, Inc., 1985), pp. 33–86.

Chapter Nine
1. Josephus, *Antiquities*, XVII, 1, 2, 15; *Wars*, I, 24, 2. For a research summary of "Polygamy" and "Concubinage," see Chapters 1 and 2 of Louis M. Epstein, *Marriage Laws in the Bible and the Talmud* (Cambridge: Harvard University Press, 1942), pp. 3–76. Of concubinage, it was described as including "any woman who had a more or less permanent agreement with a man for sexual companionship . . . [including] slave-girls and mistresses" (page 36).

Chapter Ten
1. John Bradshaw, *On the Family* (Health Communications, 1988). The ten hours of PBS video teaching by the same name is available by calling Health Communications at (713) 529-9434 in Houston, Texas.

2. Compare with Exodus 20:4-6, where "idolatry" is the sin which triggers the punishment for the offense called "hating God."

Chapter Eleven
1. Patrick Carnes, in his *Out of the Shadows: Understanding Sexual Addiction* (Minneapolis: CompCare, 1983), p. 137, offers an adaptation of the well-known "Twelve Steps" of Alcoholics Anonymous. I have made a further adaptation to identify more explicitly the distinctly Christian faith resources which more powerfully undergird rehabilitation from sexual addiction and other compulsive-damaged patterns of living.